SUCCESSFUL MIDDLE SCHOOL TEAMING

Jack C. Berckemeyer

ISBN: 978-1-56090-008-5

Library of Congress Control Number: 2022947119

Acknowledgements

Books don't just magically happen. They take time, energy, and a lot of focus—all the things I lack. I am lucky to have surrounded myself with great people who are funny and bright and hard workers. My thanks to Marj Frank for always making me sound so smart. I appreciate all the dance breaks you had to take to help make this book happen. And to Heather Roark, thanks for keeping me on the road and organized.

And thanks to:

All the schools who have allowed me to work with them to help create great teams,

All the administrators who fight to keep teaming alive in their schools,

The team leaders and teachers who work so hard to build great teams,

Paul Destino, Mark Kurz, and Kelli Cogan—three of my most enthusiastic advocates,

Chandra Juhasz, Jennifer Bicknell, and Eric Bartkowski for being great leaders and advocates for teaming,

B.J. Carson for always asking when the new teaming book is coming out,

Josie Berck McCloud—you are my sunshine on the cloudy days,

My friends who stick by me in spite of my weird personality and quirks,

And finally, to Sue Swaim, Pete Lorain, and Stephanie Simpson for continually inspiring me to be a middle level advocate.

Contents

The Power of Teaming

Teaming has truly been one of the most impactful aspects of my educational career. Being on teams taught me to be a better teacher, team player, and leader. It helped me look at teaching in a unique way; I built strong bonds with my coworkers, and I took risks that I might not have taken otherwise—in the interest of doing what was best for our students. I have been on teams of various sizes and compositions. On all these teams, we were fair and consistent, and we had fun with our students. In each case we had a principal who trusted and supported the team as we controlled our schedule and sought ways to integrate curriculum.

Teaming enriched my life! It brought me boundless experiences and memories that have lasted a lifetime. More than anything, it made me love teaching middle school. I looked forward to team time with my fellow teammates and to working with our students. Plus, I was never alone or isolated. I had others to help me with ideas and teaching strategies. I had others to support me, care for me, and hold me accountable when I became lazy or moody.

I have shed tears when a teammate has retired or changed schools. I have felt a deep sense of loss when a teammate was moved to another team. She still taught across the hall from me, yet I told her every day how much I missed her. Though I profoundly missed working with that person, I never held any grudge against my administrator for breaking up teams. To be honest, I found that the changes were helpful and kept me more engaged. A new mix of teachers challenged me to try new ideas and work with other personalities. I have embraced new team members and applauded their new ideas and energy. I have also celebrated, as well as mourned, the leaving of a team member—on occasion, even offering to pack up their stuff in order to help the move happen faster.

Yes, I have had my struggles with the adults on my team, just as I have had tons of happy times. That is all part of the amazing teaming process—the good, the bad, and sometimes, the ugly. After all, the hardest part of teaming is working with adults. The kids are the easy part.

And oh—the kids! I have seen amazing benefits to students who have been nurtured, rewarded, and empowered. How fortunate I have been to witness their successes soar in a team environment! I have watched as students have been held accountable for work, behavior, and ways they treat others. I have seen them beam with joy during special team events or reward ceremonies. I have delighted in watching them bond with their teachers and enjoy coming to school. When the students on the team are joyful, cared for, looked after, and held to high expectations, I can't help but notice that their teachers glow with high morale and a true love of teaching.

It's been a joy to see how students' families have loved and valued the teaming process. Having their child in the hands of a group of teachers who all collaborate makes communication so much more predictable and comfortable; parents and caregivers don't feel bombarded or ganged up on by teachers. They appreciate the common expectations for their child. And I have watched how they've supported teams who are open and honest about what is working for their child. I have loved hearing a parent or caregiver ask their child, "How was the team today?" (Instead of "How was school today?" Or "How was math class?"). Teaming truly helps build that bridge between schools and home.

I hope you'll embrace this book with open eyes and hearts. I hope you'll laugh at my side comments and the eccentric humor I interject. Mostly, know this: These ideas and strategies for good teaming work. They have been used, implemented, and welcomed in hundreds of schools and teams. I've watched them in action. I would not disrespect you, your team, or your school by offering things that are not effective, logical, and easy to implement. If you are doubtful about some of the suggestions or tempted to say, "But, this will never work in my school," I ask you this: "Then why does it work in so many other schools?" Give these ideas a chance. Teaming, if done correctly, will assuredly make you a better educator, foster better relationships with students, parents, caregivers, and colleagues, contribute to higher levels of student achievement, and increase your morale and passion for your job.

ABOUT THIS BOOK

The Successful Middle School: This We Believe

Since the inception of *This We Believe,* the Association for Middle Level Education's (AMLE) landmark position statement first published in 1982, middle level educators have been reading and studying the characteristics of effective middle grades schools. The document was born from a collective group of educators passionate about the concept that the learning needs of young adolescents were different than high school and elementary students. *This We Believe* quickly became an essential resource for schools that had been trying to implement the middle school model since the 1960s. It provided a true definition of the young adolescent and detailed their unique programming needs. Over the past four decades, we have seen the original 14 Characteristics of *This We Believe* grow and evolve to the 18 Characteristics outlined in the 2021 fifth edition, *The Successful Middle School: This We Believe*[1], as we continue to define how to meet the needs of young adolescents.

A key concept that emerged then and continues to be validated by research today is the importance of teaming as a core structure within a high-performing middle school. This companion guide to *The Successful Middle School: This We Believe* will help schools explore how to create and sustain a high-functioning teaming process. Ideas and strategies for school teams are tied to *The Successful Middle School: This We Believe* and linked to research and best practice. You'll find a helpful crosswalk at the beginning of each chapter connecting the element with related characteristics of a successful middle school.

Successful Middle School: Teaming

To help your school create and sustain a long-term, fully-implemented teaming process, this text identifies 16 essential elements that are critical for effective teaming. There is a dedicated chapter for each element, and each chapter answers these questions:

What? I define and explain the essential element.

Why? I describe what it looks like in schools where the element is done well—that is, how the students and other members of the school community benefit from the effective teaming implementation.

How? I give clear, practical strategies for how to put the element into action.

What to avoid? I end the chapter with some cautions about things that may derail or diminish your efforts with this element—in the form of things **not to do** if you hope to carry out this element effectively.

All these elements of effective teaming are interconnected, so the best way to start using this book is to read it in its entirety. Note that each essential action both nurtures and is enhanced by the others. They all work together to create the effective teaming process with the best results.

However, once you are familiar with the elements, you may want to prioritize and target individual elements. The book is designed for these uses too: to focus on a particular element for PD activities, to guide the work of the team for a stretch of time, or to refresh the strategies of a particular part of the teaming process in an all-faculty meeting.

ELEMENT 1

Understand What Teaming Is All About

The Successful Middle School: This We Believe
Characteristics Crossover

- Organizational structures foster purposeful learning and meaningful relationships.

Schools with great teaming begin with a clear understanding of the teaming process. They make plans and take steps to identify the benefits of teaming and the reasons it is a good choice for their school programs and students.

WHY THIS ELEMENT IS ESSENTIAL

The entire school community reaps important benefits when all members know what it means to have effective teaming, have a good idea of how teaming processes work, and look forward to the difference it will make for their students.

Here's what I see in schools where this element is done well:

- Great schools that have been implementing teaming show evidence of a deep understanding of its many facets. They embrace it!
- Across the school, there is a strong belief in the importance of teaming. The school leaders have done their homework on teaming and communicated it well to the rest of the school community. They have built a schedule around teaming as they identify and value its many benefits. (See also *The Successful Middle School Schedule,*[2] a companion guide to *The Successful Middle School: This We Believe*.)

- For schools in the early stages of teaming, there is plenty of care and preparation before the students arrive. Time is set aside for teams to create a vision, goals, and common expectations, and to get to know each other.
- Teachers have better outlooks, are more positive about the school and their students, and thrive on working together. They look forward to team time so they can come up with new ideas, flex their schedule, and find ways to connect with their students.
- Students know their school's purposes for teaming, and they know their teams well. They have helped create their team's name, motto, and identity. They have a sense of belonging and attachment to the team. They've learned the common expectations within the team of teachers, and they understand the reward systems that they helped create. They work with their peers to talk about attributes of being a good student on the team and demonstrate those attributes to the rest of the team.

HOW TO PUT THIS ELEMENT INTO ACTION

According to *The Successful Middle School: This We Believe,* interdisciplinary teaming is "a signature component of middle schooling,"[3] and, "effective teams serve as the foundation for a strong learning community."[4]

Here are some strategies for understanding what teaming is and why it is so critical to middle schools.

Know What Teaming Is

Teaming is a process that starts with a group of teachers working and teaching together with a group of students—like a smaller school within a school. These adults and kids share many common experiences during the daily tasks of school work. They form and follow consistent policies and procedures related to classroom life and academics. The members share a common mission or vision statement that allows for student input and growth. They make decisions together, all with the goal of furthering the best interests of the students. This group is a cohesive **team**. ***What***

is teaming? Here's my short definition: one group, same teachers, same students, same goals! A good team mantra is, simply: our school, our team, our kids.

The above definition is a broad description of teaming that can encompass many kinds, sizes, or structures of teams, houses, or pods formed for specific purposes. You may have grade-level teams, building accountability teams, department teams, interdisciplinary teams, cross-grade-level teams, content-focused teams, or other types of teams. The teams may be permanent or temporary. Students may be in classes within the team some of the time, most of the time, or all the time. The structure of teams will be dictated by the needs and purposes for your school. Whatever the structure, **teaming is all about the growth, development, learning, and well-being of the students.**

In this book, I focus on an interdisciplinary teaming process where students on the team are taught by the same group of teachers over a certain shared block of time and in class locations nearby one another to help with transitions and communication. Most often, these teams are made up of teachers who teach core subjects of Language Arts, Science, Math, and Social Studies. Such a plan makes for a smaller group of students learning together. It helps big schools feel small. And if your school is already small, an entire grade level may make up a team. Whatever the school size, we team to increase our communication, to become better teachers, to advocate for students, and to make sure our students succeed.

Discover and Embrace the Benefits of Teaming

No school should launch into a teaming process without identifying **why** they would do so! The "why" of your efforts is foundational to successful teaming. Here are some of the benefits of effective teaming, reasons we team—and why AMLE and I are such passionate advocates for this process.[5]

Effective teaming ...

- **Gives kids a safe, positive, and productive learning environment.** Adults and students are grouped into smaller learning communities with a sense of family. Students and teachers get to know each other well and can feel secure, supported, and willing to take risks to reach high expectations.

Together, the teachers focus on understanding and meeting the specific needs of this smaller pool of students. This helps tremendously with students' transition to middle school or high school.

- **Makes a large school feel smaller.**
  There are many large middle schools across the world, most of them in the United States, that have as many as 2,500 students. Without question, some of these schools are too large for optimal learning. *In many cases, these middle schools are so large, they could launch themselves into outer space with the energy and hormones that are produced within the walls of that building.* Remarkably, teaming creates small, personalized learning communities in any school. This gives students many of the benefits of a small school, even within a big school.

- **Increases student advocacy.**
  Teachers really get to know the students as individuals and as a group. They share responsibility for each of their students and work together to provide the best experience and support for every kid. In addition, great teams identify one special adult (an adult advocate) to have a particular focus on each student. The team sees that no student is left on the edges. *In so many learning settings, some students are overlooked because the needy, naughty, and nice students dictate where we spend our time and energy. Teams keep that from happening.*

- **Contributes to higher levels of achievement.**
  Full implementation of interdisciplinary teaming, with ample common planning time, increases effective classroom practices. The partnership of effective practices at the team level and classroom practices in individual classes can significantly boost student achievement. Moreover, the longer good teaming structures exist in a school, the greater the effects on achievement. Teaming allows for a greater focus on academic growth as teachers collaborate on the learning needs, habits, struggles, and progress of each student. A student's adult advocate pays special attention to the assignments, homework, and challenges. The team doesn't let students fall behind. Great teaming can translate to greater academic success for the students.

- **Helps students and teachers make curriculum connections.**
  Teachers collaborate across content areas. This enables them to see connections among content areas and broad concepts. Students benefit from applying the same skills to different topics and disciplines. Teachers can coordinate lesson plans to complement and strengthen student experiences in different content areas. ***Now, more than ever, we need to break down the content bunkers and seek ways to connect our curriculum.***

- **Paves the way for teachers to share and hone the best teaching and learning practices.**
  Teachers work together to find and try the best approaches for their group and for individual students. This maximized collaboration is a fantastic boost for excellent instruction and for the success of each student.

- **Elevates the sense of school connectedness and belonging.**
  Students experience the satisfaction of being part of a group and of working together in a climate of unity. The team setting enhances students' sense of belonging, helps them feel more at home in their school, and contributes to each one being a valuable participant in the life of the school.

- **Builds closer relationships and strengthens social skills.**
  A team provides a social setting more conducive to building teacher-student relationships and peer relationships. It's a context where the same group of teachers and students are better able to work consistently on getting along, working together, and valuing one another.

- **Provides consistency for teachers and students.**
  Teachers and kids enjoy consistent (rather than scattered or conflicting) expectations and procedures. Kids know what to expect. Teachers aren't contradicting other teachers' requirements. Parents and caregivers are less confused because there are fewer protocols to remember.

- **Nourishes greater connection and involvement for parents and caregivers.**
  The teaming context offers families greater comfort and sense of belonging and more frequent contacts (especially positive contacts). With an adult advocate for each student, families find it easier to communicate and to serve as engaged

and valued partners. Teaming translates to stronger partnerships with parents and caregivers and higher rates of family participation in school processes.

- **Gives teachers a sense of support and camaraderie.**
  Teaching can be a lonely venture when kids come and go but the teacher stays in the same room ***(unless you're one of those "teachers on a cart")***. Schedules and responsibilities are so non-stop that the adults often have little time for planning, sharing ideas, or socializing. Teaming is built on true collaboration where teachers enjoy shared responsibilities, grow together, and have one another's backs. Teaming improves the work climate for teachers and results in greater levels of job satisfaction. It combats burnout and contributes to higher rates of teacher retention.

- **Inspires professional sharing and growth for teachers.**
  Teams offer natural opportunities to learn from each other and grow together. Professional development is more energizing, engaging, and beneficial when team members can do it together.

Think Beyond Middle School

Teaming is blossoming in middle-level programs all over the world. These groups focus on kids, curriculum, and professional development. They find ways to meet with students as individuals and in small groups (in addition to their whole-group classes) on a regular basis. They create and follow their own discipline plans. They discuss and connect their curriculum across content areas. They spend time crafting individualized academic and behavioral support plans for students. Teams form and follow consistent protocols for classroom and academic procedures. They work continuously to improve instructional strategies, relationships, classroom management approaches, and many other actions and understandings to become better middle school professionals. ***Basically, teams come together to engage in fun, exciting, and relevant learning experiences.***

Many elementary school and high school educators and students also work and grow in some sorts of teams. These groups meet to discuss student data, work on educational plans, correlate curriculum, meet with students or parents and caregivers, and learn together. Many high schools have also adopted some kind of teaming process, with special attention to the needs of first-year high-school students in such programs as freshman academies. Schools have seen great results in improved academic outcomes and increased graduation rates.

Because teaming is such a strong component of an effective middle school program, we often think of it solely as a middle level concept. However, it is also a smart idea for students, students' families, teachers, and administrators of all levels. The goal for any school should be to figure out the best way to make sure teachers have time to meet and work together in their teams. Between ever-increasing need for attention to students' academic, social, and emotional needs and greater accountability for meeting all these needs (by the way on limited budgets), teachers need team time more than ever.

Great schools know the value of teaming. They've seen proof that effective teams jointly serve as a solid foundation for strong learning communities. Effective teaming of any structure or grade level offers the kinds of benefits described above for students, teachers, and schools. But no matter what grade levels are included, schools often struggle to know how to organize the kind of teaming that is best for them and to make sure that teams use their time together effectively and carry out the right actions to meet their teaming goals. The proven (and amazing) benefits of teaming make it worth the struggle to learn about teaming, boldly take the actions needed to do it well, and put it to work in your school.

Do Your Homework

Don't start teaming without these: learning and training! One of the most troublesome facts about teaming efforts in schools is that quality training for leaders and teams, though absolutely essential, often gets left in the dust when the next new initiative comes along.

Before beginning a teaming process, learn as much as you can. There are hundreds of articles, books, videos, blogs, and experts to teach about teaming's foundations and processes for effective teaming; plenty of exciting research supports the benefits of teaming. Investigate the research; share it with your staff and school community; visit schools where teaming is working well; have long conversations with teachers and leaders who are experienced in teaming; and train with teaming experts. Assess the needs of your school, staff, and students. Identify aspects of teaming that will make a difference in your setting. Find people or programs that will specifically help train your leaders and staff to get a good teaming process underway.

Effective teaming requires ongoing attention long after the start-up process or beginning of the school year. It needs continuous work, care, learning, training, evaluation, and modification. There is no "getting to perfection" in your teaming process. Schools with great teams change and grow each year—adapting to different students, teachers, and needs. And above all, great teaming needs time—ample time for team members to plan, problem-solve, and grow together. Each year, the teaming can become more and more of a wonder with multiplied benefits. Research shows that the improvement in teaming practices and classroom practices which lead to higher achievement are most evident when schools have implemented effective teaming for two to four years of more.[6]

AVOID THESE ACTIONS

In this chapter, you've read about what to do to put Element 1 into action. Here's a quick list of some things **not** to do.

As you work to **understand what teaming is and why to do it**, steer clear of

1. Starting or continuing teaming because you have to, rather than because you believe your school needs it.
2. Neglecting to do the research and homework to learn about good teaming.
3. Implementing teaming without adequate, quality training.
4. Failing to fully embrace the benefits that teaming offers your students and school.
5. Setting processes without basing them on the needs of **your** students and **your** school.
6. Leaving all decisions about your teaming processes in the hands of one leader.
7. Letting yourself be swayed by the presence or demands of powerful doubters.
8. Backing down from the fight against budget restrictions or unreliable financial support needed for great teaming.
9. Forgetting that teams and administrators need ongoing training after teaming is implemented.

ELEMENT 2

Get Everyone on the Same Page

The Successful Middle School: This We Believe
Characteristics Crossover

- A shared vision developed by all stakeholders guides every decision.
- Professional development for staff is relevant, long term, and job embedded.

Schools with great teaming build the teaming process on a solid, common vision and mission that is developed collaboratively and supported by all the stakeholders within the school. In order for everyone to speak the language of teaming, leadership teams, teachers and other staff members, students and their parents or caregivers, school and district administrators, the board, and the wider community must be able to articulate the true purpose of teaming.

WHY THIS ELEMENT IS ESSENTIAL

The entire school community reaps important benefits when all the people affected by teaming pull together behind the teaming process to agree on the goals, purposes, and structure and commit to good communication and full support.

Here's what I see in schools where this element is done well:

- Educators work together to create the teaming process. Input and ideas are solicited from and generated by all stakeholders.
- Teachers and leaders have received relevant, long-term, and job-embedded training in teaming processes.

- Everyone in the school knows the value of teaming—and enthusiastically shows it.
- A meaningful and easy-to-understand school teaming mission and vision is created and shared with the school community.
- Teams have set goals and expectations with student input and have shared them with everyone on the team, including students and their families.
- Administrators empower the teams to make decisions that are in the best interests of the students.
- The teaming structure includes ample and regular common planning time.
- Teaming has a set time, purpose, and structure. This allows teams to work together to support students and families.

HOW TO PUT THIS ELEMENT INTO ACTION

Here are some great ways to communicate your school's teaming mission and make sure that everyone affected by teaming embraces and advocates for the teaming process.

Review the Definition and Benefits of Teaming

When you launch your plans for getting everyone on the same page, begin by sharing your definition of teaming. Use the definition from the section "Know What Teaming Is" in Element 1 on page 2 of this book. Or use a definition you have previously chosen for your school's teaming process. Distribute and discuss the definition. Solicit questions, feedback, and ideas from the various parties affected by teaming. Think about what makes your school and your teaming process unique. Then hone your definition to one that has consensus.

Also share the evidence-based benefits of teaming, such as those shown in the section "Discover and Embrace the Benefits of Teaming" in Element 1, pages 3-6. Help all stakeholders understand that the extent to which students (and others) gain the benefits of teaming depends on the effectiveness of the team. The far-reaching effects of great teaming multiply as teams have more common planning time, more experience working together, and fuller implementation of such proven, excellent teaming practices as: increased family engagement and involvement, cooperation with other resource staff in the building, and coordination of curriculum, student assignments, assessments, and feedback on their academic progress.[7]

Don't start or continue a teaming process until everyone affected by it has clarity about what teaming means, along with appreciation of the fantastic benefits of teaming done well. This knowledge sparks everyone's energy for the next steps in implementing this element.

Create a School Mission and Vision for Teaming

In a school with great teaming, leaders embrace the wide spectrum and diversity of people who are affected by teaming. They work collaboratively with all stakeholders to build a mission and vision that describes the what, how, and why of their teaming commitment. Most schools already have a mission and vision statement for the overall educational program. For assistance in creating that mission and vision, see *The Successful Middle School Schedule,*[8] a companion guide to *The Successful Middle School: This We Believe*. An all-school teaming mission and vision statement derives from your overall school mission and vision. It is somewhat different, however, in that it is **specific to teaming**.

The ***mission*** part of the statement describes what and how of the process. It focuses on the present purpose or beliefs or actions, and it answers such questions as:

- *What does our teaming process do or provide?*
- *What is the purpose of our teaming process?*
- *For whom is this provided?*
- *How do we do this?*

The ***vision*** part of the statement focuses on the future—what actions we hope or intend will be the results of following our mission. It answers such questions as:

- *Where are we headed?*
- *What will we do next?*
- *How do we intend to grow?*
- *What changes do we envision from where we are now?*

When you choose to institute a teaming process, teaming becomes the heart of your school culture. A culture is the personality of the school—the underlying beliefs and values that shape every aspect of the school, including the relationships within it and all the ways things are done. It influences and permeates the experiences and actions of all members of the school community.

A strong school-wide mission-vision statement presents teaming as intrinsic to the school culture. It becomes a guide and basis for decisions about the shape, goals, and purposes of the teaming. It also serves as a foundation for teams as they develop their individual mission and vision statements, philosophies, or goals.

A few more bits of advice for this task:

- There are many possible strategies for crafting this statement. One approach is to use a 1-2-4 process, which begins with individuals drafting a statement. They then join in pairs, and the pairs join into fours—each time creating a version upon which they agree. Groups of four share drafts with the whole group, which works together to find consensus on a final draft. For a guide to this process, see Resource #1, "The 1-2-4 Process: Ways to Reach Agreement on Just About Anything," on page 189.
- When you have multiple middle schools in your district, each school's mission, vision, or philosophy will be different. There is no one correct way to design such a statement. Yours should be as unique as your school and the people in it.
- Make sure that students are at the center of your mission-vision statement.
- Craft statements that are concise, readable, and make good sense to all parties. Avoid statements that are lengthy, boring, or loaded with trite phrases and educational jargon.
- Share copies widely—with teams, students, parents and caregivers, all staff members, leaders, district board members, district administrators, and district constituents. Post this on the school website, district website, or both. Find other easy and creative ways, as well.
- Actually use the statement. Keep it handy for reference in all further steps of planning, organizing, and evaluating teams and teamwork. ***(Don't bother writing one if you're just going to stash it in a file somewhere.)***

- Check on yourselves often to see if you are faithfully following your teaming mission and working toward your vision. Regularly ask yourselves and other stakeholders: *Did we further our teaming mission-vision today? This week? With this activity?*
- Re-visit the statement. Schools with effective teaming will regularly request that all parties review and add input to the statement and revise it as needed.

There are philosophical vision and mission statements for teaming that are wordy and only created to check a box of completed items in the teaming process. Some of the best statements about teaming relate to the climate and culture of your school.

For example:

At Berckemeyer Middle School, teaming is an opportunity for a group of teachers to be creative, flexible, innovative, compassionate, and fun so students can learn to be successful in school and life.

At Central Valley Middle School, we believe that our young adolescent students thrive and learn in safe, personalized learning environments where each one feels a sense of belonging and receives individual academic focus and support.

Therefore, we choose and implement an interdisciplinary teaming process where teachers make connections among skills and concepts across subject areas, have common expectations for behavior and procedures, and appoint a specific adult advocate for each student. We will schedule and protect ample common planning time for teams to discuss student, team, and instructional issues, and meet with parents or caregivers and students.

Agree on Your School's Goals for Teaming

Goals for teaming flow naturally from your mission and vision. Teams will form their own goals to fit their individual situations and settings. Here are some sample school-wide teaming goals:

Give our middle-level students safe, family-like learning environments.
Increase belongingness and school connectedness for our students.
Offer continuous, personalized support to each student's academic success.
Find and use better instructional strategies for our students.
Build close, trusting relationships among peers and between teachers and students and their families.
Provide learning settings appropriate to the students' early adolescence developmental stage.
Integrate curriculum and learning skills.
Promote better and more frequent connections with families.
Learn and expand the use of evidence-based teaching practices.
Increase active and project-based learning.
Enhance support for social-emotional learning.
Learn from each other.

Note: You may even create some funny goals…

Not pop a gasket when we get 20 emails on the same day from one parent or caregiver.
Not roll our eyes when a teammate talks about how awesome her cat is.
Not giggle when a teammate says the word dongle, climax, or talks about Uranus.

Decide on the Right Teaming Structure for Your School

Your teaming goals, and the accomplishment of your mission and vision, are interconnected with your teaming structure. And structures of teaming are as varied as the schools that pursue a teaming process.

Some of your structural decisions will be dictated by forces beyond your control. You'll have to work within the larger school and district programs. You'll have to fit your teaming plans with school schedules, physical layouts, space, and budgets.

A complete structural plan will include:

time and places for training in teaming processes
team configurations
grade level(s)
student mixture
number and kinds of content areas
number of teachers
combinations of teachers
classrooms and other locations for classes
how much of the school day students will learn in teams
how the schedules will work
times for team planning meetings

Note: For many teams, having 85% of your students taught by the same teachers on that team is considered a pure team of students. With the influx of so many high school credits being pushed down to middle school, it is hard to create a team where the teachers have 100% of the students for all their classes.

Think about how other teachers and content areas—outside of the teams—will work with and support teaming. If you already have teaming underway, this will be a process of re-examining the structure and adapting it to improve teaming and to fit with changed personnel or circumstances. The wonderful thing about getting a workable structure in place is that you can make it better every year that you continue teaming.

Absolute necessities in making these decisions are:

- Include representatives from all stakeholder groups in this process.
- Keep the needs of students at the forefront of decisions.
- See that your choices further your mission and vision for the teaming process.
- Do what works for your school—don't think you have to replicate another school's structure.
- Build into the plan adequate time and places for the administrative team to collaborate with teams.

- Build into the plan adequate time and places for teams to plan together.
- Build training for teachers *and* leaders into the plan.

I want to emphasize the last two points above:

1. **Common planning time for teams.** This is the heart of effective teaming. Research affirms that schools with high levels of planning time (ideally four meetings per week of at least 30 minutes duration) have the highest levels of solid teaming practices and have the strongest influences on effective classroom practices (for example: active small-group instruction; integration of disciplines; authentic assessment; and critical thinking, reading, writing, and math skill enhancement).[9]
2. **Training for leaders and team members.** Lack of training harms the processes of teaming. Many schools and districts will say that they've had training for teaming—yet it was, like, ten years ago! New research and practices have become available in the interim and new teachers have been hired; but they have not been trained. ***They're just expected to "pick it up" from colleagues.*** Over time, bad habits in teaming practices might have become entrenched. If you've been teaming for a while, ask yourselves this: "When was the last time we provided professional development around creating quality teams and using quality teaming practices?" "Ten years ago" is not an acceptable answer!

   Let's be realistic. It costs money to have a teaming process. So while we have to demonstrate that teaming is a value of our school through the dollars we spend, there are also many cost-effective ways of providing current and quality professional development for our teams, team leaders, and administrators, including both in-person and an online (for example, see AMLE's online teaming course at AMLE.org).

   Some teams do a self-surveying team assessment to see how they have grown and to analyze what they need to improve. I have been lucky to work with hundreds of teams over the years. Some schools choose one-day in-services, while many others are plan for multiple days so that teaming experts can meet with each team during their team time. This eliminates the need to hire substitute teachers and is extremely effective. And it saves money. Whether you choose in-house training, online training, or training with an outside consultant, don't start or continue teaming without an ongoing professional development strategy in place.

There is no one, ideal structure for teaming—no one right leader personality, team configuration, mix of team members, or exact grade levels. There is no "best" schedule or sacred, set list of protocols for all teams. There are dozens of human, organizational, and financial variables. The best structure for you is the one that fits for your students and staff—the one that works to accomplish your purposes and goals for teaming.

Plan for Informing All Stakeholders

When making decisions about the mission or vision, purposes, goals, and structure of teaming, plan ways to let everyone know what's happening. It's not likely that every single member of the school community will take part, physically, in the final decisions about all of the above matters. Don't end your planning or begin your school year of teaming without providing a full, understandable strategy to everyone involved.

Agree on and distribute informative messages that are clear, meaningful, and concise. Make sure these communications showcase your belief and passion for teaming. You want each member of your audience(s) to be fired up about teaming. Take care to make all messages available translated into languages as needed for your stakeholders.

Plan for Continuing Buy-In from All Stakeholders

Yes, getting everyone involved, informed, and excited at the beginning of the process, or again each year, is essential. But excitement can dwindle. People can forget why they're doing something or why you are doing something. Other programs or needs can begin to seem more important. Funds can get diverted elsewhere.

Be realistic about waning enthusiasm. Plan ways to keep the buy-in from everyone who benefits (even when they forget that they are benefitting). The best way is to have an effective teaming process. But even then, some stakeholders may not notice the benefits unless you bring it to their attention. You'll need to actively and continuously boost the whole-community belief in teaming and commitment to the unique teaming processes in **your** school or district. Here are some ways to do that:

- Share real samples or testimonials about how teaming is positively impacting your school. These could be positive teacher, parent, caregiver, student, or leader experiences with the teaming process.
- Show evidence (hard data) of improvements in achievement, behavior, attendance, dropout rates, and teacher retention resulting from the teaming process. Show the reductions in failures.
- Offer teams examples of how they can be flexible with their team time.
- Give all stakeholders ideas for how they can continue to be actively involved in the teaming process.
- Use all media and available communication channels to showcase team activities and accomplishments. Explain how they further the teaming mission, vision, and goals. Reinforce the ways that teaming is foundational to the culture of the school and the school community.

AVOID THESE ACTIONS

In this chapter, you've read about what to do to put Element 2 into action. Here's a quick list of some things **not** to do.

As you work to **get everyone on the same page,** steer clear of

1. Giving into the temptation to skip or spend too little time on this element—thinking it's too hard or not important.
2. Failing to use a democratic process to get meaningful input from all stakeholders.
3. Getting derailed by uncooperative or obstructive participants (instead of finding ways to entice them into the process).

4. Caving in to overbearing administrators pushing their views onto the group.
5. Smoothing over questions or issues that arise, leaving them unresolved.
6. Forgetting to communicate—in writing—the final mission, vision, and other parts of the teaming process with the wider school community.
7. Becoming lax about KEEPING everyone on the same page over the long haul.

ELEMENT 3

Nurture and Sharpen Leadership

The Successful Middle School: This We Believe
Characteristics Crossover

- Leaders demonstrate courage and collaboration.
- Professional learning for staff is relevant, long term, and job embedded.

Schools with great teaming need courageous and collaborative leadership. This includes all leaders involved in the process—the school principal (or other administrator) or administrative team that oversees the teaming process for the whole school plus the individual team leaders.

WHY THIS ELEMENT IS ESSENTIAL

The entire school community reaps important benefits when time and attention are given, not only to choosing the right people for leadership positions—but also to supporting them as they cultivate the skills needed for their particular leadership roles.

Here's what I see in schools where this element is done well:

- Schools that thrive with teaming have great administrators who become strong advocates for the process. These administrators advocate for teams and support them with their actions, policies, and voice. They speak up at the district level meetings to assure financial allocations are made to support the teaming process. They especially speak up to combat the erroneous view that teaming is just an extra planning period and not productive team time.

- The administrators provide to school boards and other leadership teams the quantitative and qualitative data that demonstrate how great teaming practices are making a positive difference. They accommodate team time in the master schedule—and vigorously defend the need for ample team time. They work with others to help inspire the passion for teaming and seek out great team leaders.
- Team leaders motivate and energize the teams. They are the backbone of team; the teaming concept flourishes in their care. The teaming mission and vision is alive and evident. Team leaders work with team members to effectively use their team time. They are carefully chosen and, ideally, compensated for their role as team leader.
- Parents and caregivers see a cohesive, purposeful teaming process with knowledgeable leaders at the helm of the school and the teams. Students know that teaming is an all-school priority—not just important within their individual teams.

HOW TO PUT THIS ELEMENT INTO ACTION

This group of suggestions will help in the choosing, training, and nurturing your teaming administrator to oversee the school's teaming as well as designating and training team leaders.

Build Effective Leadership at the Top

Teams, and the teaming concept, can flounder without an administrator who is an advocate in each school. When a leader in this position waivers, caves, or does not build the capacity to grow teams, the teaming process has little chance of success.

It's not an easy task to maintain long-term teaming dedication and development. New initiatives come along all the time. ***About the time you get everyone on the same page, that page gets ripped away and a new chapter replaces it!***

It is imperative that district personnel, including the superintendent, school board members, and curriculum directors, support the school administrator and the teaming concept. To do this, the district personnel, too, must know the importance of the elements of teaming.

Every school administrator (in a school with teaming) needs comprehensive team training. The person in this role of overseeing the school's teaming process must be able to provide input and advice and lend support to help teams succeed. Even schools that have been teaming for years should have intensive follow-up professional development at least every few years. District administrators must understand the need for this training and lend support to their school-level leaders. They must facilitate and fund this training and stand behind the school administrator and team leaders with commitment and action.

Consider Personal and Leadership Qualities Needed for Teaming

Here are some personal qualities and commitments to look for as you consider who have leadership roles in your school teaming processes. These apply both to the school administrator and the leaders of the individual teams.

A good administrator or team leader:

- Believes fervently in the teaming process and is passionate about taking on a teaming leadership role.
- Is trained for teaming or eager to get as much training as possible.
- Can work well with and motivate others in a respectful and collaborative manner.
- Values others; works at trusting, caring relationships.
- Welcomes diversity; can work with all types of personalities and talents.
- Remains highly alert to personal bias of any kind toward any persons or groups.
- Has an optimistic, enthusiastic attitude.
- Identifies, champions, and values the contributions and talents of others.
- Can make difficult decisions in a fair and timely manner.
- Can share leadership and responsibility.
- Regularly asks for feedback about their own working style, attitudes, and decisions.
- Operates with transparency, is calm and steady, and takes calculated risks.

Clarify the Job Description for the School's Administrator

If the school leader shows little appreciation and understanding of the elements of effective teaming, teams will lose focus. At worst, teamwork meetings will become venting sessions for frustrated educators. The administrator who oversees a school's teaming process must constantly be on the lookout for ways to support these elements and help teams put them into action. Great school administrators know the essential elements for effective teaming and work tirelessly to make them happen!

A great administrator

Fulfills the following roles:

- Keeps the school's teaming mission, vision, and goals firmly in mind at all times.
- Sets the tone for teaming by being extremely knowledgeable about the teaming process.
- Acts as chief ambassador, communicator, and braggart about the teaming processes in the school—including benefits, activities, and accomplishments, and shares that good news with school boards, community members, and district staff.
- Advocates heartily for adequate team planning time and provides training for teaming.
- Spends time with all the team leaders; checks in often to see if they need advice or support.
- Provides new ideas and resources to support teams so they grow in their instructional practices.
- Regularly (monthly or so) sits in on a team meeting for each team. For a tool to guide team observations, see Resource #2, "Administrator's Checklist for Team Observation," on page 190.
- Uses a checklist of actions for effective teaming as talking points to see that teams are implementing elements of teaming.
- Helps teams stay on track and use team meetings wisely. (See Elements 5, 6, and 7.)
- Reviews team meeting agendas now and then.
- Reviews each team's calendar; encourages teams to share the calendar with administrators and other teams; and keeps a check on student workload for the week.

- Becomes familiar with each team's processes for student academic intervention and support.
- Becomes familiar with each team's discipline processes, interventions, and behavioral supports.
- Coordinates connections among teams and between teams and other teachers and staff members.
- Makes and follows plans to help struggling teams, and follows up on progress.
- Works with teams to develop a system for team assessments (common to all teams).

Understands that Teams Need:

- Flexibility during the core time to be creative with their schedule. Yes, this might cause frustration for the main office personnel. But kids can be located by teachers on the team when they move students around.
- To be able to work with special education and essentials (electives) teachers when being creative with core time. This also means that the team must communicate well with these teachers about possible changes.
- To be able to create team identity and rewards systems for their kids—in most cases using students to create those components and rewards.
- Freedom to create an easy-to-use system to access when entering and reviewing communications with parent and caregivers. (As an alternative to individual teachers recording parent contacts, this will be done by the entire team.)
- To be allowed to bring students into team meetings for pep talks or to discuss grades, behavior, or needs. Teachers need training as to how to conduct such meetings.
- Freedom to create their own agendas for their meetings.
- To be able to call on resources as needed—such resources as the principal, counselors, the resource officer, and other support staff.
- Freedom to explore creative options for helping individual students succeed in their content areas.

- Freedom to create academic or behavioral plans or interventions for their students.
- Flexibility to connect curriculum in ways that might not specifically align with the prescribed curriculum.
- Encouragement and flexibility to try new instructional strategies.

Not only will the administrator step up to the above tasks and support the above needs of teams, but they will also assure, honor, and reward teams when they are moving in the right direction and, when necessary, help teams "shape up" and get back on the right path. Without this leadership and strong internal support, outsiders may question why teams are important to successful schools.

For some superintendents, school board members, and other teachers in the district, there is a perception that the cost of teaming in a school is not necessary. This is not a new argument. Such critiques typically include:

It's just another prep time for teachers.
*I wish **I** had more time to do nothing.*
Half of those teachers don't even like each other!
What are teachers really doing in those teams?
Why are teams spending 95% of their time on the same 5% of their students?
Does teaming really affect academic achievement?

In some cases where a team is not using its time effectively, these questions and comments are valid. And in some instances, schools need to make the necessary changes within teams. But individual cases of ineffective teams do not invalidate a practice with a wealth of research that supports its positive impact on kids. Yes, sometimes teams struggle. But that can be fixed and is uncommon when there is a teaming administrator who acts as a true advocate for teaming.

Yes, that's quite a sizable job description! There's a load of serious responsibility there. But there's plenty of joy and satisfaction in doing this job well. It leads to truly effective teaming. And, here's something I've witnessed again and again: Just as this leader boosts teaming, so effective teaming bestows a multitude of blessings on the administrator. This person benefits from:

1. More communication directly between teachers and parents or caregivers.
2. Greater school connection with students' families.
3. Handling of minor discipline issues by teams, saving the administrator hours of managing discipline.
4. Consistency in teacher expectations for students.
5. Reward systems that work better with high student involvement in their creation.
6. A wealth of creative and effective ways that teachers increase student academic success.
7. Better communications and greater comradery among teachers.
8. More team-handled solutions of parent or caregiver and student concerns and issues.
9. Increased student voice and choice.
10. The security of every student having a specified adult advocate.
11. Better teacher morale because they feel empowered to make decisions.

Clarify the Job Description for Team Leaders

One of the most critical roles in teaming is the team leader. The team leader is the pulse and energy of the team. The best teams I have ever worked with have had strong, hardworking team leaders. These folks also have had ongoing training on how to be a team leader. They know how to work well with others and, when necessary, can take control and lead the team in tough decisions. Not all educators are up to the job of facilitating team meetings and keeping the team on task. Thus, these leaders must be carefully chosen, developed, and nurtured.

Team leaders must share in the vision of teaming and be excited to be part of a team. Their selection as team leader should not be based on losing a battle of Rock, Paper, Scissors. Team leaders are rotated after a couple years or at a semester break. They are not kept just because the team members think they are great. ***In many cases, that just means the others on the team don't want the job. The more highly the team leader is praised by their teammates, the more likely it is that no one else wants to be team leader.***

The hardest parts of being a team leader are staying organized, keeping people on task, and dealing with conflict when necessary. ***At times it's a bit like herding cats.***

There should be an application process for a team leader! They need to know the expectations and the role they have in the teaming process. I struggle with the issue of paying team leaders a stipend. I am old-school: I'm from the era where my principal used to take the team leaders to a conference, such as a state-wide or AMLE middle school conference. That was our reward for the extra work. We got free travel, hotel, and lots of food. I thought it was better than the extra $31.71 per pay period for being a team leader. I have changed my mind since then: if it's possible, then yes, it is wise to have a stipend for team leaders. As always, that depends on the district policy and contracts.

A great team leader

- Knows, encourages, and facilitates the essential actions for effective teaming, including the team vision, norms, goals, and purpose.
- Teems with enthusiasm for teaming and always keeps the team focused on students.
- Leads well, but shares responsibilities with other team members.
- Upholds and empowers all team members, and identifies and appreciates contributions of each one.
- Comes to meetings ready to offer ideas, but does not overpower others with their ideas.
- Actively shows respect for other members and for kids and their families.
- Keeps open communication with other team leaders, teams, and staff members outside the teams.
- Helps the team take on and navigate new strategies and processes.
- Helps the team make hard decisions with confidence and conviction.
- Guides the team in following through on what they decide.
- Is prepared for roadblocks and setbacks; helps teams handle failure and use it for growth.
- Leads the team meeting with a clear agenda and makes sure the teams meet regularly (or sees that another member is ready to lead a meeting).

- Makes meetings fun.
- Keeps the team focused on the big three priorities: kids, curriculum, and professional development.
- Sees that all members can speak and be heard at team meetings.
- Is avid about not wasting team time.
- Brings in resources to help team members build instructional excellence.
- Guides and challenges the team in self-evaluation and growth.
- Arranges for professional development to benefit the team members.
- Sees that all team decisions and accomplishments for the meeting are summarized at the end.

Although one member may have the designation of team leader, all members must take responsibility for leadership functions. Leadership may flow, depending on the task at hand. A good team leader invites and facilitates shared leadership. Every member is an equal part of the team and has equal power and accountability in the process of meeting the team's goals. Equal participation should be a given.

Plan for Initial and Ongoing Leader Training

No individual should step into any leadership position in the teaming process without training in the teaming concept and the essential elements of effective teaming. This includes the school administrator and the leaders of individual teams. There are many ways to provide training. It can be a combination of one or more of these options—the more, the better:

Reading, listening to, or observing good teaming research and information
Visiting schools where effective teaming is in process
Taking part in workshops and seminars
Receiving training from consultants skilled in helping schools with teaming
Attending a conference on teaming or holding your own conference and inviting other local teaming leaders

Whatever the training, don't start teaming without it. Plan ahead of time. Don't wait until the last month before school starts.

One small, or even large, dose of teaming instruction is not enough. Teaming leaders need periodic training seminars plus regular, ongoing experiences with teaming professional development. They need collaboration with other leaders in the process of teaming. They need feedback from stakeholders, discussion sessions, self-reflection, and learning experiences with the teachers in their schools. There are dozens of ways for leaders to keep getting better at leading. The longer a school engages in teaming, the more the educators learn about what more they need to learn! See that this periodic leadership training is part of your teaming plan and budget.

AVOID THESE ACTIONS

In this chapter, you've read about what to do to put Element 3 into action. Here's a quick list of some things **not** to do.

As you work to nurture and sharpen great leadership, steer clear of

1. Making leadership choices without taking seriously the school's cohesive vision and purpose for teaming.
2. Failing to provide training specifically focused on good teaming leadership.
3. Getting derailed from sharpening leaders by apathy or skepticism from the "higher-up" administration.
4. Giving into pressure from "higher authorities" about whom to choose as leaders.
5. Choosing a teaming administrator who is not thoroughly committed to teaming.
6. Assigning team leaders by seniority.
7. Being shy about campaigning for adequate resources to support the teaming process.
8. Neglecting to set up adequate time and systems for communication and support between the administrator and team leaders.
9. Allowing too little time in the schedule for the school and team leaders to do their jobs well.

ELEMENT 4

Carefully Create and Organize Teams

The Successful Middle School: This We Believe Characteristics Crossover

- Organizational structures foster purposeful learning and meaningful relationships.

Schools with great teams take an astute, well-planned approach to how they will place teachers on teams for the result of strong, productive teams that are the best possible places for the students to learn.

WHY THIS ELEMENT IS ESSENTIAL

The entire school community reaps important benefits when leaders are thoughtful, knowledgeable, and meticulous about assigning teachers to teams, organizing teams, and making changes in team composition when needed.

Here's what I see in schools where this element is done well:

- Administrators don't treat the responsibility to create and organize tasks as a simple administrative task. They anticipate and plan for a multitude of factors that must be explored and discussed in the process of creating teams. The sharp teaming administrator takes time and calculated risks to wrangle with competing priorities, including mandates, certifications requirements, standards, and curriculum configurations to find a process for creating and organizing teams well.
- The administrator shows wisdom and skill in making adjustment to teams—which is sometimes needed, even after crafting the best teams. People

move or take other jobs, or personality issues develop that harm the team's productivity. When these things happen, changes are imperative. I see sharp administrators who act with courage to rearrange teams, knowing that the goal is to produce a team whose members work together effectively to do great things for students.

- The teachers know how their teams were chosen and organized. The process was not shrouded in mystery, so they feel comfortable and trust in it. They are empowered because their opinions, suggestions, and ideas were welcomed. They can see that great care was taken in the creation of the teams.
- Students benefit from the conscientious, purposeful approach to setting up teams. They gain value from the variety of teaching styles and talents of the carefully-chosen team members. They get a comfortable start to the new year when their teachers and leaders are confident about their teams. Individual students are likely to have their needs met from the strong teams.

HOW TO PUT THIS ELEMENT INTO ACTION

One of the hardest tasks an administrator will do in their educational career is to create teams. In many cases this can be a lose-lose situation. It can be frustrating and even result in a few gray hairs ***(or a total loss of all hairs)*** over the long ordeal. However, with some time and energy, great administrators can work out all the pieces and thoughtfully align teachers to form amazing teams.

The following strategies will help administrators with this challenging task of shaping the best possible teaming combinations.

Decide on the Make-Up of Teams

Who will be on the team? Who will not? Again, based on the school's teaming needs and structure of the teaming process, the answers to these questions will vary. Consider these examples and possibilities:

- A teacher for each of the content areas covered by the team
- The placement of an elective (essentials) teacher on the team

- The addition of a reading-literacy teacher
- The addition of a special education teacher
- The addition of a foreign language teacher
- The potential of students being cross-teamed due to classes offered at higher levels
- The removal of the math teacher (See a fuller discussion of this new concept on page 37.)

Think Ahead About Strategies for Creating Teams

Just as there is no one sacred team configuration, so there is no one perfect way to create teams. In most cases, the more input you elicit and the more people you involve in the process, the better. But at some point, after gathering information and viewpoints, the decisions have to be made! Here's some advice; take from it what is useful in your situation.

- Survey the staff about whom they would like to work with for the next several years. Make sure they justify their answers. Just as when middle school kids are placed in group learning situations, it is not about "being with a friend."
- Ask why they would **not** work with a certain faculty member. It's important to do your best to identify situations in which certain combinations will not work. So, take these responses seriously. Reasons need to be based on philosophical issues or, in rare cases, on unresolvable personal issues. For example, one teacher may note that they have a similar instructional style and practices as another teacher, and suggest that it would be more beneficial to students to have teachers with more diverse approaches so the team meets the varying learning styles of the students. ***Because a teacher once ate another teacher's yogurt is not a philosophical issue.***
- Map out teachers' certification areas and grade-level certifications.
- Chart teaching strengths and select teams based on these strengths.
- Chart personality strengths and areas of growth.
- Don't let teams get too large.

- Create smaller teams for younger grade levels. When possible, fifth or sixth grade teams should have two to three teachers. This helps students with transitions between classes.
- Decide how to involve the electives teachers (or, I as call them, *essentials* teachers) and teachers of other content areas as part of the teaming process. Some middle schools choose to create an essentials team. However, this can create a scheduling issue. If creating an essentials team is difficult due to traveling teacher issues or part-time teachers, at least consider an essentials team with the essentials teachers who are there all day. You can even create smaller essentials teams based on the schedule and classes. There could be a technology team and an arts team. The essentials teams could be grouped into humanities, fine arts, and applied arts teams.
- Sometimes it's not workable to include an essentials teacher, literacy teacher, or special ed teacher on each team. Remember that there are many ways teams can connect with and be supported by these teachers without having them as official team members.
- *Check astronomy charts to see if teachers are aligned. You may need a little something strange to help put the last pieces together. Maybe ask your Yoga teacher for their advice. The family pet may even have a few thoughts. Joking aside, this is a hard process! So, in most cases, go with your gut feeling.*

Change or Rearrange Existing Teams When Necessary

Changing or rearranging a team means adding a new member to a team, replacing a member, or moving a member to a different team. Sometimes this involves more than one member. There are several reasons for doing this: The most common is that a teacher has changed jobs within the school, moved to a different school, retired, or left teaching altogether. Or there may have been a decision that another member should be added to the team—perhaps a special ed teacher, a fine arts teacher, or an essentials (electives) teacher.

Other reasons might be less straightforward. They might come down to this—the team just cannot stay as it is! When teams are not working together and become divisive and unproductive, school leaders will need to isolate the problem and make changes in the membership. Or if the teams have divided themselves from other teams and become competitive with each other, then changes are needed. My friend Kathy Hunt-Ullock, a long-time teaming advocate and brilliant trainer of teams, once shared this:

> *I find that, in many schools, some teams that have become institutionalized are highly competitive with each other. For example,*
> *One eighth grade team might have a unit on zoology.*
> *Another team steps up and says, "We are going to the zoo!"*
> *Another team tops that with, "Well, we are bringing in Jack Hanna."*
> *And the last team simply says (with a smirk), "We are going to Africa!"*

The rule of thumb is that teams need at least three to five years to really come together and make progress. It is not until year seven that teams start to take on the biggest personality. In some cases, that big personality may not be positive, and then suddenly the whole team becomes negative or toxic. When this happens, action must be taken for the benefit of the students, their families, and the adults on the team. The action may be moving a team member or two to another team or swapping a team member with another team.

Making changes in teams takes courage and finesse. Leaders will need to be honest, direct, and confident in taking this step. They must come to this decision (and present it) with carefully-considered and articulated reasons—reasons based on facts, not just hearsay. It's important to prepare well for the discussion in which this action will be presented.

For administrators who are thinking about moving teachers around on teams, consider these questions:

> *Why am I doing this?*
> *Are all the teams in the building working effectively?*
> *Are the teams meeting their own goals and the school teaming goals?*
> *Have any of the teams taken on a negative personality?*
> *Is the reason for changing the teams to hide a poor or inadequate teacher?*
> *Is there an unhealthy team (overly competitive or chronically underperforming)?*

Are the team dynamics harmful to students? If so, how?
Will the changes increase student achievement? If so, how?
Will the changes improve teacher-student relationships? If so, how?
Will the changes improve peer relationships? If so, how?
Will the changes increase family involvement? If so, how?
What do I expect will happen with the changes?
Have I already done everything in my power to help this team with whatever issues bring me to consider a change?
Do I have substantive evidence for the reasons for doing this?
Do I really want to do this?

Evaluate the answers to these questions before you take the giant leap into the wild world of changing up teams. This leap can truly make or break a school environment and cause a lot of stress on school administrators.

Then, if you are still certain that you need to proceed,

1. Have clear documentation (situations, examples, etc.) for your reasons.
2. Make a plan for how you will proceed.
3. Consult with the team members on why changes need to be made.
4. Solicit retirements. ***(Just Kidding!)***

Dismantle Teams When Necessary

Sometimes, as administrators, we have to ask ourselves: "How are **all** our teams functioning?" or "Is this team, or this whole grade-level of teams, in trouble?" In some cases, teams become dysfunctional to the extent that trading out a member to another team is not enough of a solution. When this happens, we must ask: "How do we dismantle the team?" This is not easy for a leader. By *dismantle,* I mean, to break an entire team apart and find other teams or places for them. It may also mean removing some of the teachers from the teaming process altogether, assigning them to teaching duties outside of teams.

Great leaders will start the dismantling process early by attending some of the team meetings to try to identify the source of the tension and negativity. The leader will talk with each team member individually, asking such questions as:

What is hurting this team?
Is there a way to fix the team?
What changes would you make to this team?
How do you think dismantling a team will affect the teachers (and students) within this grade level?
How will you react if changes are made?

In all cases, being honest and direct is the best policy. School administrators have to ask the tough questions to arrive at what is best for teaming in the school. They also need the courage to actually remove someone from the team and away from a teaming position. This will mean that maybe a team is missing its science teacher because that person has been given another duty during the team-meeting time.

Another reason for dismantling a team or changing your overall teaming concept relates to the practice of adding so many higher-level math classes into middle schools. This has a huge impact on student composition of teams—and it makes it hard to have multidisciplinary teaming at all. Have we recreated the horrible notion of tracking? The middle school concept has always included a commitment to heterogeneously-grouped teams. Adapting the team configuration to have a grade-level math team (or teams) and a team with high school math challenges the idea of heterogeneous teams. Have we walked away from that belief in favor of pushing high school credits down into middle school?

One solution is to remove math from the team content areas and offer it in an elective format. This could result in more math options for students without creating advanced and standard math teams. This is a huge discussion with massive ripple effects within the school and teams. However, letting high school credits dictate or alter our middle school concept might not be what is best for our students. It's an issue worth tackling and solving!

Whether the change involves adding a new member to a team, rearranging members between teams, or dismantling and restructuring a whole team (or more), spend time preparing the staff. Make these decisions before the end of the school year so that teams have ample notification and can start making necessary changes. Explain the reasons and process well. Change can be very hard for the teachers, and many may remain bitter for years unless they are part of the process and are well informed during the decision-making process.

Always know that making team changes can be full of mistakes and challenges, and can have a negative impact on the school; but it can also be the breath of fresh air that is needed for the students and teachers.

AVOID THESE ACTIONS

In this chapter, you've read about what to do to put Element 4 into action. Here's a quick list of some things **not** to do.

As you work to **create, organize, or change teams,** steer clear of

1. Playing favorites in team assignments.
2. Being secretive about who's on which team.
3. Yielding to outside pressures about your choices.
4. Skimping on the time it takes to explain your choices.
5. Letting fear keep you from confronting problems that demand team change-ups.
6. Forgetting to include teachers in hiring new team members.

Element 5

Take the Leap and Become a Team

The Successful Middle School: This We Believe Characteristics Crossover

- The school environment is welcoming, inclusive, and affirming for all.

Great teams commit to building a healthy, well-functioning team. They put in the work to create a sense of shared community for the joint purposes of the best possible academic, social, and emotional climate for the students. Even if the team has been together for a year or several years, a great team starts anew each year at committing to a harmonious, productive group relationship.

WHY THIS ELEMENT IS ESSENTIAL

The entire school community reaps important benefits when all the teams in the school energetically collaborate to get to know each other and invest in planning, teaching, growing, and nurturing students together.

Here's what I see in schools where this element is done well:

- Teachers enjoy being with their teams. They laugh a lot. It's obvious that they have spent time getting to know each other and agreed on ways to get along.
- Team members accept the varying personalities, talents, and quirks of one another. They show trust in and respect for each other.
- Teams have crafted a thoughtful statement of their beliefs, philosophy,

or mission. They share and discuss this with their students. They use this statement as a foundation for their work together.

- Teams take ownership of the team and show a high degree of support for each other and for group processes. Members see themselves as equal partners in responsibility for the success of the team and the students.
- Students learn better. The harmonious, cooperative interactions among the teachers translate to comfort, stable operations, and student success.
- Students are offered good models for respectful working relationships.
- The school teaming administrator supports and nurtures the efforts for teams to come together and forge their unique personalities and philosophies.
- Because the teams in their school function smoothly, administrators have fewer worries and headaches.

HOW TO PUT THIS ELEMENT INTO ACTION

Get to Know Each Other

Healthy team building begins with members getting to know one another as people and as educators. Once a team is created, members need time together. This step is not just for new teams, but also for teams that have been together—even for several years. Great teams will meet in the summer prior to school. They might meet at a member's house or a local gathering place ***(preferably one with easy access to food; everyone loves a Bundt cake or a cupcake.)***.

It is critical for teams to set aside time to talk about things not related to school. Later, there will be plenty of opportunities to worry about progress reports, team celebrations, and who needs to bring doughnuts to the next team meeting.

Here are some ideas of what to do for the first meeting. ***Do this even if the team has been together for a while. People's lives change. New stuff happens. Each year, you'll learn fresh things about each other.***

- Spend time talking about your teaching background.
- Talk about some of your teaching strategies.

- Share your pet peeves.
- Talk about family and why you became a teacher.
- Share a great past teaming experience, or describe a great teaming experience you hope to have this year.
- Create a list of non-negotiables you expect from your teammates and yourself regarding your team for the next school year.
- Conduct and share a fun survey—not too serious. *Cosmopolitan* magazine always has interesting surveys **(although you might not want to know if your team member is a member of a biker bar).**
- Keep the first meeting lighthearted and have plenty of food.
- Remember my motto: Eating makes a meeting!
- Share a photo of yourself as a middle school student. Maybe talk about your struggles, triumphs, and experiences during those middle school years.
- Some teams list their degrees and other individual or group accomplishments to post in their team area of the building. We should be proud of the hard work we have done and of the many hours we spend outside of the classroom increasing our knowledge. Don't neglect bragging about these!

One great way to start the process of team bonding is to do something that will get you laughing. I love to see all teams start off by all completing a slightly wacky "getting-to-know-each-other" questionnaire. There are two in the resource section at the back of the book. But these are just examples; you will certainly have even more fun adding other questions to these or completely concocting your own. See Resource #3, "Getting to Know Your Teammates" on page 191 and Resource #4, "Do You Really Know Your Teammates?" on page 192.

Think About Who You Are As a Team

I have been lucky to work with hundreds of interdisciplinary teams in my career. I have seen great teams, functioning teams, marginal teams, teams that should be broken up, people who should never be allowed to work with other adults, team members who poo-poo dreams, team meetings run by administrators because the team members can't get along, and teams that just tell stories, gossip, vent, and never get anything done.

I have witnessed good behaviors and bad behaviors by team members. I've seen teams where members care for and support each other during tragic times, celebratory times, and times when they just needed some humor and love. I've watched and heard team members say dreadful things to co-workers—comments from which neither will ever recover. I've witnessed temper tantrums by grown adults, passive-aggressive behaviors, mean looks, walk outs, and crying. As I mentioned in the introduction to this book—dealing with adults can be the hardest part of teaming!

Over time, teams tend to develop their own personalities. Most often, they settle into patterns that have wonderful and productive aspects. But sometimes, there are features that wear down members or interfere with the best outcomes of teaming. This development of teams' unique styles or "flavors" is an inevitable part of the teaming process in a school. Here are a few of the team types I have discovered:

> **The Overachievers.** Every school has a team that embraces new ideas, tries inventive practices, and takes risks. Usually, as soon as the principal announces a new idea or initiative, this team is all over it. They are inspired and energized; they love the idea of teaming. These teachers have posters that embrace their team's name or motto. They have matching shirts and dress alike on random days.
>
> This team laughs, enjoys school, and loves their students. They plan fun rewards, have special days for their students, celebrate birthdays, and look at teaming as a great opportunity—definitely not as a burden or just another thing to do.
>
> One issue for the overachieving team is burnout. Though they are motivated, without ample recognition from administration and others they can feel unappreciated and overworked. Yes, they need a pat on the back and loads of appreciation.
>
> **The Effective and Efficient Team.** There is absolutely nothing wrong with an effective and efficient team. They look at teaming as a checklist. They

pride themselves on accomplishing as much as possible. This group of team members is competent and focused; they look at teaming as a task that needs to be done and as a key part of the school day. They get things done! This team has a pleasant nature, and they work well together.

The effective and efficient team usually has a great team leader who keeps them focused and on task. The leader prioritizes what the team needs to do. The team offers various rewards and plans special days for kids—but only if other teams are doing special days or rewards. Team members regularly take notes during team meetings and are the first team to realize that no one else reads those notes. So that keeps them slightly discouraged about some of the elements of teaming.

However, at some point, a team member will have a breakdown when the tasks seem too overwhelming. They will start to question some of the tasks. They will feel frustrated about things beyond their control and sometimes ask, "Why are we doing this?"

The Fun-but-Forgetful Team. This is the team that wants to turn the library into a space station. They get very excited, have ingenious ideas, will try anything—yet have little follow-through. They laugh during team time, maybe even sharing funny videos or memes with each other. They tell a lot of amusing stories about their kids and each other.

The fun-but-forgetful team likes the idea of doing cool things with kids, but collectively lacks the ability to see things through. They also struggle with holding each other accountable to task. People love being on this team.

Their struggle is to complete tasks: They start off strong and end in frustration. In many cases, they lack a great team leader who will hold others accountable. They know they need to establish team norms, but because they don't want to hurt anyone's feelings, they never get around to doing so. When conflicts occur within the team, they struggle with how to confront the issues.

The Marginal-but-Meaningful Team. This team thinks a lot, talks a lot, discusses a lot, ponders a lot, and sometimes comes to a decision. They have opinions on a multitude of things. Most of these things have nothing to do with teaming. Many are items, issues, and concerns beyond their control. They are easily disillusioned and give up quickly on trying to find solutions.

This team is unsure of its place within the school. Members question many decisions that come from district-level administrators. They're likely to say, "We get no support from our administrators when we have a problem."

This team is capable of doing great things as a team; but they get caught up in the "uncontrollable bubble" (meaning, they are so focused on things they can't solve or control, that they become frustrated and just give up.)

The marginal-but-meaningful team often has fantastic ideas. Lacking the commitment to make changes, the great ideas go nowhere. They like the status quo. They complain and want someone else to solve their issues. This can be hard for a new teacher who has just joined the team—the pessimistic atmosphere makes it scary for the newcomer to speak up to offer feedback, ideas, or solutions. One serious pitfall for this team is that, too often, they allow the most negative person to dictate the culture of the team.

The Pick-a-Little-Talk-a-Little Team. They have a lot to say. The talking starts from the minute they walk in the room and carries on until the bell rings. At the end of the team meeting, they wonder what happened to the time. Almost always, someone says, "I wish we had more time." They mean well but just lack focus and a solid team agenda.

This team struggles with structure. The members need to create action items, have a time keeper to keep them on task, and stick to an agenda. They could move all their talking time to the end of meeting and set up a positive structure for their team time. But they haven't worked at such strategies.

Sooner or later, a team member will get tired of the gossip and scatteredness and will shut down, retreating into silence. This will lead others to be concerned that, now, there is conflict in the team. In many cases, they will ask that person, "What is wrong?"

The response will be, "Nothing. I am just fine." What an unfortunate response—just when this would be a great time for that person to speak up and say, "Can we please stop with all the needless gossip and idle chit chat, so we can get some real teamwork done?"

For this team to grow, the members need someone to be courageous and challenge the status quo and the unhealthy patterns established by the team.

The Tense Team. From the moment you walk into the presence of this team, you can sense the tension. This group of adults can't find ways to get along. Or they just don't like working with each other. They harbor bad feelings, or they are just angry about all the things in the school or in education that they can't control. I have sat in on many painful meetings where it's clear that things have been said in the past that have poisoned the atmosphere indefinitely.

Here are some comments said in team meetings (I've heard them!) that are hard to recover from.

> *I don't care what kids do in other classes. My class is the most important.*
> *I have seen the work you give kids and none of it is rigorous.*
> *You can all decide on whatever you want. I am just not doing it.*
> *I am tired of speaking my truths in the team meeting and having some of you run right to the principal's office.*
> *I told the parent that I am the only one on this team who cares about kids.*
> *None of my teammates do anything.*
> *I don't trust any of you in this meeting.*
> *I don't respect people on this team.*

Please note that these were all said out loud and in front of the team. Imagine the list of things said behind each other's backs! Trust me: the list could go on and on. Unfortunately, and all too often, the tense team has no desire or ability to change the feelings of animosity. Some team members just seem to take pride in making things awkward for others. There are ways to confront and find solutions for such an unpleasant working atmosphere. I've shared some thoughts about solutions in the following section, and more in Element 7, where I discuss norms for team meetings.

The best teams have a combination of many attributes. My hope is that teams embrace varied characteristics and behaviors and find the appropriate times to hold the administration accountable; to debate an issue; to create rewards for students; to listen to each other, uphold each other, and cry or grumble with each other; to vent about kids; to brag about kids; to have fun; and, especially, to laugh with each other.

Make it a goal, as a team, to ask the question: "What kind of a team **are** we?" Stop and reflect on your team's personality and patterns. Put these into words. Write them down and take a good look at them.

Also make a point to consider this question: "What kind of a team do we **want** to be?" Put these ideas in writing. Compare these to your answers for the previous question. Doing this together will give your team a chance to commit to changing patterns or starting new behaviors as needed.

Agree to Work on Getting Along

There is much work to be done by teams. Schools, students, and families are counting on teams to take teaming seriously and do it well. But it's impossible to be fully effective at teaming if the group can't get along. As you build or reinvigorate your team in a new year, take time to discuss the factors and behaviors that make up a good working relationship for your team. This is not yet about how to run meetings, what to accomplish in meetings, or what goals to set for students. This has to do with decent ways to **be** with one another and **treat** one another for the end goal of the best possible educational experiences for your students. And while you're choosing what's good for the students, you'll also be choosing a satisfying, productive working climate for yourselves—one of the best ever professional and personal experiences!

Make some simple promises for working together in ways that are agreeable, satisfying, and even joyous. Having such commitments to one another provides a strong foundation to fall back on when situations or team members get difficult.

The team can refer to these to remind themselves how they agreed to treat each other and work together. The list does not have to be long—but it should be **your** list of must-haves for getting along. The list may include such straightforward items as shown below:

We will

Believe that positive collaboration will lead to improved learning and classroom life for our students.
Treat each other respectfully.
Be kind.
Believe that each member is an important part of the team.
Welcome and appreciate individual personalities, styles, and talents.
Listen to each other in ways that make it safe to express opinions and ideas.
Communicate honestly, openly, and directly—no hidden messages.
Be flexible, not rigid.
Trust each other, and be trustworthy.
Honor confidentiality and privacy.
Not hold grudges.
Meet obstacles and hard choices with optimism.
Get teamwork training together.
Laugh together.
Eat together.

Be Aware of What Hurts Teams

We know a lot about what helps a team function smoothly. The list of practices above shows some of the characteristics of a great team. To the ability to work together respectfully and productively and have good communication, positive attitudes, and lots of fun, joy, and laughter—add these: creativity, patience, willingness to take risks, and fervent belief in teaming concepts. All are marks of ideal working relationships! But we should also be alert to some things that seriously hurt teaming and upend efforts to work well together. These are circumstances I must mention.

Teaming is truly hurt by

Educational sabotage. You might not find this term in a college textbook, yet it happens all the time within the school walls. It happens when teachers meet with teachers and when principals meet with teachers or parents and caregivers. It happens in faculty lounges. What is it? It's a situation in which someone says something negative about another person in order to make the person look bad in front of others. As my good friend and long-time school administrator, the incredible Judith Baenen, once said, "Teacher bashing happens all over; the worst place is within the school walls."

Educational sabotage is a power grab that plays out between people when someone chooses to use information, comments, or actions to demean, embarrass, or weaken another person. We might think it's harmless gossip or that we are just joking around. But it's not harmless. It's no joke. It has tremendous negative effects on school culture and climate. And it's deadly for team dynamics.

If members of the team talk outside of the team about their teammates, it creates a very divided team. Teachers lose trust in each other; people feel used and betrayed. It is hard enough to deal with a world of negative teacher bashing from parents and caregivers, social media, and television. It is even harder when we do it to each other.

Another form of sabotage is when we share outside of the team discussions and decisions that are confidential to the team. Even if there is no intent to demean a team member or the student, family member, or colleague concerned—this is a betrayal of trust with our team members. It undermines are work together. One person's gossip or inappropriate sharing reflects on all the team members, making the whole team look untrustworthy.

Advice: Teaming needs to be like Vegas: what happens here stays here. And secondly, start your first team meeting by agreeing to ban educational sabotage in any form.

Takeover by the strongest personality. Sometimes the most powerful personality dictates the mood of a group. How many of us know who the power broker is in our own families? For example, you may have an older sister whose voice is heard louder than other siblings. Or an uncle's opinion is always the final decision-maker in the family. In each case, these family members have the greatest influence and the biggest personality. And they very often have the bossiest effect (or stranglehold) on brainstorming of ideas, controlling others, final decisions, and determining how things are done.

The same can be said for teaching teams. The teacher with the quietest voice may not be heard or have their opinions taken seriously. We tend to listen to the person who is bold and, in many cases, opinionated. And maybe even a bit scary. They can control the narrative, the decision-making process, and the mood of the team.

If the boldest team members view all decisions from administration as a negative thing or an annoyance, the team is likely to feel the same way. Meetings become a feeding frenzy of negativity. But the opposite is also true: if the strongest team personality is all roses and sweet candy gumdrops, then the team can take on those attributes.

Great teams assure that everyone's voice is heard. Yes, this is easier said than done. Usually, we simply ask if everyone is okay with the decision, topic, or process. Most people either don't respond or give only a slight shake of the head. With this minimal engagement, it appears that everyone is okay with it when, in actuality, some or all may be either too timid to disagree or just tired of fighting against the strong personality.

Advice: Great teams see that each person is asked individually what they like about the plan, process, or decision and what they might question or struggle with. This encourages everyone to have a voice in this process. And it forces the chronic non-listeners to listen to their teammates.

A drive through Uglyville. If teams don't spend time listening to each other to solicit opinions from every voice, team dynamics often take a turn for the worse.

This can happen out of the blue, or during a full moon, hot day, or right before grades are due: A teacher will snap! The anger from months of being ignored or pushed around will fester up, and the person will lose it. This usually involves slamming their palms on the desk and re-slamming after each syllable—while they are talking. I have seen it. They just get fed up! The emotional response might be over a student, a new idea, or a change to their daily routine. Sometimes, things are said, and the person is just angry and needs to vent.

Advice: Now and then, even on great teams, a "breakdown" gets out pent-up feelings. But what hurts a team is the inability to have tough discussions without letting the process become mean, spiteful, or hurtful. It's a challenge to keep charged issues in balance with kind behavior—but we can't let a situation become toxic. If things get too intense, pause the meeting and ask that everyone get some water, coffee, or a sedative. ***Depending on the group, humor may or may not be a wise decision.*** When things calm, bring everyone back and set ground rules for how to move forward. Driving through Uglyville can actually help a team refocus, recommit, and reenergize—if given a little time and a lot of compassion.

Create a Team Mission

Near the beginning of the year, take some time to develop a team mission and vision or philosophy that reflects your team characteristics, expectations, and perhaps future goals. Make sure that this team-specific statement is grade-level appropriate. You can use the school's teaming mission and vision statement as a starting point for creating your individual team statement. There is no one ideal approach or label for this. It can be a mission or vision statement (or both), a statement of beliefs, a philosophy, or a set of goals for the year. Together with the school's statement, the teams' statements further unify the direction for teaming in the school. So, it is imperative for teams to focus on quality statements.

Note that there is no need for a formal declaration, trumpets to sound, and a banner to be flown when a team develops a mission statement. Sometimes it is as simple as asking and answering a few brief questions. Here are some examples:

Who are we as a team? How are we unique?
How do we work together?
What do we believe about teaching or education in general?
What do we believe our students need?
What do we believe about teaming?
Based on our beliefs, what do we already do for our students?
What do we want to accomplish this year?
What outcomes do we want for our students?
What will we do to make this happen?
How will we know when we have accomplished our mission, purpose, or goals?

As you collaborate to draft and hone this important product:

- Work at finding core beliefs and values. Notice what everyone is passionate about.
- Make sure everyone has a voice and is heard.
- Keep it simple.
- Review it to make sure that all components are straightforward and easy to understand.
- Present the final product however you like—for example, as paragraphs, a list, a diagram.
- Remember that this is a process; discussing and creating are as valuable as the final statement.
- Present your product in whatever form fits your statements. Just be sure to
    - Focus on this year and on the needs of students.
    - Identify the intended results for students.
    - Ensure the statement has the agreement and endorsement of all team members.

Your team statement may be a short statement of who you are as a team. Or it might be a more extensive look at your team philosophy, beliefs, or vision. See some examples of these on pages 193-195 (Resources #5, #6, and #7). You'll notice how, in each case, team members present their messages with their own flair.

Yes, you can even add some humor to your mission statement! After all, this is for **your** team. In some cases, you may want to have an official statement and an unofficial statement.

Our team is made up of veteran teachers who know how to communicate well with parents or caregivers and students. We seek ways to connect our curriculum. We provide positive rewards for our students and make sure every child is truly cared for. At the end of the year, we take time to reflect on the success of our students and how well we worked as a team.

We work on surviving every day. Once a month, we go to happy hour as a team. Our students are not invited. On the unplanned days when we all wear a similar outfit, we take a picture. It's a miracle when we all have matching socks. **(Okay—just checking to see if you still are with me!)**

Our team is committed to the academic success of each student. We believe that our students need a supportive environment for learning—that they grow when they interact with others.

Therefore, we will ascertain each student's academic needs, work thoughtfully with the student, parents, and teachers to devise strategies for their success, and regularly monitor their progress. We will create opportunities for students to work in small groups, will take measures to boost a sense of belonging for all students, and will agree with our entire team to live by common values and expectations.

When your team vision or mission is complete, do not shove it in a notebook or leave it to get lost in the abyss of hundreds of files on your computer. This statement or set of statements will be what gives cohesion to the team. It is a foundation on which to rely for making decisions and choices.

- Post it in your classrooms. (Students can make the posters.)
- Make plans for reviewing and discussing it with students.
- Share it with parents and caregivers and other members of the school community.
- Put it on your team website.
- Review it during team meetings.
- At the end of each meeting, ask yourselves, "Did we further our team mission today?" or "Did our decisions support our team philosophy?"

AVOID THESE ACTIONS

In this chapter, you've read about what to do to put Element 5 into action. Here's a quick list of some things **not** to do.

As you work to **become a healthy, well-functioning team**, steer clear of

1. Neglecting to take enough time to get to know each other.
2. Failing to identify the gifts that each teacher brings to the team.
3. Overlooking conflicts or issues without confronting and working them through.
4. Gossiping about team members or sensitive team matters outside of the team.
5. Creating a team philosophy or vision that is too long and complicated.
6. Forgetting the need to discuss the team mission and vision with students.
7. Ignoring (not using well) the mission and vision once it's created.
8. Allowing the difficult team members to have their way, just because it's easier.
9. Letting your team slide into patterns of unkind and contentious behavior.

ELEMENT 6

Plan for the Hard Work

The Successful Middle School: This We Believe
Characteristics Crossover

- Organizational structures foster purposeful learning and meaningful relationships.

Great teams know what the important work of the team is and commit to full implementation of teaming processes. They understand the benefits of effective teamwork—the improved outcomes at many levels, for students, parents or caregivers, and teachers.

WHY THIS ELEMENT IS ESSENTIAL

The entire school community reaps significant benefits when all teams in the school understand what it means to fully implement teaming practices, know the specific tasks teams can and should do, and have formed clear plans for how they accomplish the work.

Here's what I see in schools where this element is done well:

- Teams and leaders take seriously the importance of the work teams must do, and they get the work done.
- Team members know the specifics of the work that great teams do.
- Teams plan how to spend their time by choosing where they will focus their energies. They don't spin their wheels trying to accomplish everything at once.
- Teachers work together from a common understanding about where they are in the list of teaming practices, and where they want to go.

- Teams are comfortable making decisions together. They've planned ahead for tough decisions that will come up.
- Leaders appreciate the independence and competence of team decision-making.
- Students are clearly the key focus and purpose of the teams' work.

HOW TO PUT THIS ELEMENT INTO ACTION

The more fully teaming is implemented, the greater are the benefits. Full implementation means consistent and effective application of **team-level practices**. When this happens, the results are a better learning climate for students, higher levels of student achievement, more frequent contact with and involvement of parents and caregivers, an improved work climate for teachers, and increased job satisfaction. In addition, regular success at team-level activities has strong, positive effects on pivotal instructional practices carried out in the individual classrooms of the team.[10]

Know What a Team's Work Is

In a nutshell, the work of the team focuses squarely on these three priorities:

- Kids
- Curriculum and instruction
- Team professional development (strengthening teaming and teaching practices)

These are your major umbrella items that stay in the spotlight! But let's look at some of the activities that flow from these core priorities.

The work of the team includes these tasks:

- Use common planning time effectively.
- Monitor each student's academic performance and progress.
- Keep eyes on each student's social and emotional well-being.
- Advocate for each student and for the team of students.
- Attend to building and sustaining team identity and unity with students.
- Coordinate curricula and instructional strategies.
- Use, share, and learn excellent instructional practices.

- Coordinate student assignments, assessments, and feedback.
- Keep a team calendar that coordinates schedules.
- Keep regular contact with students' families.
- Find ways to build trusting, caring relationships with students and their families.
- Plan and implement strategies to increase parent and caregiver involvement.
- Contact and coordinate with other building resource staff.
- Set consistent expectations (across the team) for academic work.
- Set consistent procedures for meeting classroom expectations.
- Set consistent grading policies.
- Create and follow a team-wide discipline process.
- Find and use a multitude of good ways to boost student academic success.
- Develop and use a strong student-support action plan (for academic, social, emotional, or behavior needs).
- Establish norms for teamwork and team meetings.
- Meet as a team with students.
- Meet as a team with parents or caregivers.
- Keep records that document all team actions, decisions, and contacts.
- Regularly reflect on and self-evaluate the success of the team's work.
- Include frequent and targeted professional development for the team.

The team's work should be primarily accomplished during designated team time. Decisions made in team meetings set responsibilities for who will do which portions of the work—and when and where. The team's success depends on good working relationships (see Element 5), commitment to regular team meetings, and efficient use of team common planning time. (See more details about team meetings in Element 7.)

Build a Base for Planning the Work

If you've started and continued the processes of bonding as a team (Element 5), you've had fun getting to know one another, agreed on your team mission and purpose, and committed to some actions and attitudes for working well together. In addition to these steps, teams must build baseline data about their team structure, the focus of their work, and the effective use of time.

For existing teams:

During the first few weeks of school, existing teams should work together to complete the two-page self-check survey, "Where Are We Now?" (See Resource #8 on pages 196-197). This allows the team to gather information about the current state of various team policies and practices. Responses will indicate areas for team discussion and will guide your priorities for how to use your work time. (Please note: There may be some strategies you feel you do not need. Just make sure you review and discuss them as a team.)

If, as a team, you discover areas of weakness or identify missing strategies, create goals for your upcoming teamwork. Feel free to add questions that relate specifically to your school or team, or to substitute your own questions for some on the list.

For new teams:

If you're just beginning to work together as a team, you won't have had enough time to progress to the third or fourth column of the table. However, completing the survey together will still be a valuable team activity to help you set goals for your teamwork and consider how you will spend your team time.

I encourage teams to take this informal survey at least twice a year. All team members will find it interesting to see how well the team is accomplishing its work near the beginning of the year in comparison with the middle or end of the year. Keep track of the data from your surveys. (See Element 14 for more information on documentation and Element 16 for a deeper discussion of team reflection.)

Administrators can also review the "Where Are We?" surveys to keep track of the practices that teams are implementing or developing. This is not a checklist of things that every team must do or a complete list of all possible team tasks. Present this to teams as a list of some of the practices and ideas that many teams are implementing for effective teaming.

Set Priorities for Your Teamwork

It's obvious that teams have plenty of important work to do. But you can't do all the jobs at once. Yes, there is ongoing work that continues throughout every day and during all team meetings. Many of these are tasks that have to do with monitoring and supporting students. The self-survey outlines tasks that, if not already completed and implemented, can be prioritized.

The survey results and a review of the teamwork items listed above can guide your work. They will help you decide which aspects of your teaming need tweaking, which need greater reworking, and which tasks or products you have not yet started. As you move to prioritize these, ask

What is the best use of our time?
What is our major focus?
What do we do first?
What is most urgent?
What are our goals for this week (or month or quarter)?
Which can we complete in one meeting?
Which tasks can we split into smaller pieces for individuals to do?

Agree on your top priorities. These goals will be valuable guidelines as you plan your individual team meetings. (See the next chapter, Element 7, for greater detail about using team-meeting time to plan and accomplish specific teamwork.)

- Use a team planning calendar to plot out goals for a month, quarter, or year. It will be a general plan, identifying documents, policies, or norms you'll need to create or polish.
- Decide what is urgent. What sets the stage for classroom operations and expectations common to the team? What policies help students feel welcome, oriented, safe, and unified? Take care of these early in your teamwork schedule.
- For each task you set, be clear about what you will do, who will do it, and when it will be done.
- Remember the umbrella priorities. The work of the team is about the kids, the curriculum, and team professional development.

Agree on Your Decision-Making Processes

The fact is, I am not sure we will ever have complete consensus on any issue or task in education. The reason? Educators can be strong-willed and opinionated. These characteristics are admirable, and needed at times! But at other times, we must all work together to find common ground.

For a person like me, making decisions in collaboration is difficult. I see things the way I see them. At times I can be aggressive and assertive. I tend to not want to back off on my position. I can even beat the dead horse until it is reincarnated! So, for me, consensus is not an easy process. This is also true for many other educators. Coming to consensus is a struggle. (Do you have a Jack Berckemeyer on your team, or more than one?)

The various personalities on a team translate to a variety of ways of reaching a conclusion. This makes team consensus a challenge. Take these differences into account as you choose a decision-making model for your team. Here are some typical personalities that teams need to consider as they choose their consensus mode:

The Thinker. Thinkers take time to consider options and ramifications. They process all the information and try to reach a solid decision. This could take anywhere from a day to 52 weeks.

The Quick-to-Judgment Person. These teachers have an answer right away. They have made up their minds until someone convinces them otherwise. They voice their thoughts immediately, yet can talk about the issue forever.

The Waffler. Wafflers see every side of the story (including sides no one could ever have imagine existed) and can never come up with one answer. They make statements like, "Well, if we do this..."

The I-Don't-Commit Person. These people do not want their names next to anything. They don't like to take risks, and in many cases, did not even hear the question.

The Dazed-and-Confused Person. These folks are in the media center waiting for the meeting that started 20 minutes ago in the science room. So, they are no help in decision making.

The Simple-Solution Person. These teammates just appreciate when someone looks them in the eye and asks, "Well, what can you live with?" How many times in your career have you wished that someone would just ask you what you could live with? It is better than someone trying to verbally beat you down with more examples and laying on a guilt trip about how you don't care about kids. Knowing what a person can live with is a great starting point for moving toward a decision upon which all can agree.

No matter who your team members are or what their inclinations are about working out agreements with others, the team will have to make decisions together. So, it's imperative that your team considers what the decision-making process will be—and do this early—before a big crisis pops up. This way, you have something to rely on other than giving up or giving into the loudest or most stubborn voice!

Researchers and educators have developed many great models for making decisions. See Resource #9, "Some Decision-Making Models" on page 198 for a sampling of ways to approach making decisions together.

In general, a decision-making process includes such steps or components as these:

1. Identify and define the problem.
2. Gather information to verify that the problem is defined correctly.
3. Discuss (and agree on) whether this is a real issue that requires a decision.
4. Set a climate that allows for all members to comfortably state their views.
5. See that everyone takes part in the discussion.
6. Develop alternative solutions.
7. Identify consequences (positive and negative) for each alternative.
8. Listen to each other (one person talks at a time). Summarize what has been said.
9. Choose the BEST alternative for the desired outcome.
10. Clarify what action will be taken and who will take it.
11. Follow through. Implement the decision.
12. Evaluate the outcome *(Did you reach the desired effect? What worked?)*

For an organizing tool that guides you through the steps of decision making, see Resource #10, "Anatomy of a Decision." on page 199.

Great teams explore ways to make decisions together and establish a process that works best for them. Here are some suggestions for going about this:

- Understand that **how** the team decides is as important as the decision itself. Making decisions together is a superb learning experience for teams.
- Recognize that each team member has different styles and comforts (or discomforts) related to group decisions. Get to know these differences and respect them. Use a decision-making process that honors this diversity.
- Be proactive about team consensus building and decision making. Don't wait until there is a crisis. Try out some models and practice them.
- During a team meeting spend a few minutes role-playing a "decision needed" scenario. Approach the scenario as if it were a decision that your team needed to make immediately. Discuss the scenario and decide what your team would do. Then reflect on your team's decision-making process. Try to identify what happened. Give each team member time to reflect aloud on how they felt about the process, whether their voice was heard, whether they agree with the outcome, and what they might have done differently. This activity should provide insight into the way your team makes decisions. Use this insight to create a plan for addressing real decisions.
- Work together to make sure every decision the team makes is filtered through the question: *Does this meet the needs of our students?*
- You don't have to use the same decision-making model every time, but do have a couple in your team repertoire. Vary which model you use, depending on the kind of decision.
- When setting the team decision-making process, don't forget to agree on how the final decision is made! Do you look for group consensus? Do you take a vote? I think it depends on the issue. For small, low-impact decisions or issues, you might simply take a vote—using the "majority rules" approach. For bigger decisions, consensus is desirable.
- Consensus doesn't necessarily mean unanimous agreement. Of course, it's great if there is unanimity. But often, not everyone prefers one option. In

these cases, the final decision may be an agreement you can all live with—what you can support.

- Once made, everyone needs to stand behind the decision and help implement it.
- Include after-decision reflection as part of your process. It's not practical to do this every time, but once in a while—particularly with the most major or difficult decisions—review what you did, how you did it, and how it turned out. Ask a few simple questions such as

  What happened?
  Did everyone get and take a chance to be heard?
  Did we gather and consider important facts and background information?
  How did we reach the decision?
  Did we all agree with most or all of the decision?
  Did the decision focus on what was best for the student(s)?
  Did the decision support (not compromise) our beliefs? values? mission?
  Did we act on the decision? Did we all help implement it?
  Did the decision accomplish what we hoped?
  What went well in our process? What did not go well?
  Do we need to try a different decision-making approach?

The importance of working out ways to make decisions and resolve conflicts cannot be overstated. The experiences and process around making the decision will have longer-lasting effects than the decision itself. **By the way, if you're brave enough—hold a mock team meeting in front of your students. Show them how you make a decision together. It's a great way to teach them the process!**

AVOID THESE ACTIONS

In this chapter, you've read about what to do to put Element 6 into action. Here's a quick list of some things **not** to do. As you focus on **identifying and doing the work of the team**, steer clear of

1. Not fully appreciating the widespread effects of team-level practices done well.

2. Having an incomplete idea about what work the team needs to do.
3. Failing to stop and evaluate where you currently are in the progress of your teamwork.
4. Overlooking the need to choose areas of focus for your work.
5. Trying to do everything (from any list of team tasks) at once.
6. Forgetting to keep the best interest of the kids at the forefront of all choices and plans.
7. Neglecting to choose and practice a team decision-making process.
8. Clinging to the idea that every team member must be thrilled with every decision.

ELEMENT 7

Don't Waste Team-Meeting Time

The Successful Middle School: This We Believe
Characteristics Crossover

- Organizational structures foster purposeful learning and meaningful relationships

Great teams treat their common meeting time as sacred. They plan and operate tight, efficient, effective meetings so that none of the precious time is wasted.

WHY THIS ELEMENT IS ESSENTIAL

The entire school community reaps significant benefits when teams have adequate common planning time, know the value of their time together, and consistently make every minute count to achieve their goals for their teaming practices and for their students.

Here's what I see in schools where this element is done well:

- Teams get better and better at teaming as they spend more quality time planning and working together. Teachers are energized after team meetings. They learn new things and grow together.
- Teachers become familiar with the rituals of teaming as they begin to see their work together take shape and their teams build unity. They enjoy the benefits of the organizational improvements with their team calendars and joint communications with parents and caregivers.

- Teams know where they are headed in each meeting. They follow a clear agenda and are productive.
- Teams make headway on such important processes as starting and keeping a communication log and a team calendar, creating common procedures and expectations for themselves and students, connecting curriculum and instruction, and designing common rewards for students.
- Teams have assigned team leaders who make sure teams meet consistently, guide quality meetings, and see that teams evaluate their work regularly.
- Good planning and organization from team meetings translates to better classroom management and teaching in the individual classrooms.
- Families experience frequent communication and clear information from the team.
- Students have more consistency in classroom routines and practices stemming from the joint planning by their teachers.

HOW TO PUT THIS ELEMENT INTO ACTION

Keeping everyone focused during team meetings is, by far, one of the he hardest parts of the teaming process. There can be tons of school-related and personal interruptions. We can easily wander off task—distracted by a hot topic, email reminder or text notification "ding," or a shiny object. Because we are educators who spend most of our lives with children or adolescents, when we are with semi-mature adults, we tend to want to take time to vent, complain, or just relax and catch our breath. All of this is normal and fine; it just can't take up the entire meeting (or even a large chunk of it).

Make Commitments About Why and How We Meet

The team meetings are the settings in which many of the important teaming practices are followed. This is where the essential work gets done. It's critical that members of new and existing teams make or refresh commitments about what will happen at the team meetings. Early on in your life as a team, or early on in a new school year, discuss these two facets of your team meetings.

1. **The reasons for this group of teachers to meet.** Ask each other: "Why do we come together to meet frequently?" Give everyone a chance to provide a reason or two. You may hear such answers as:
   - ◇ *Talk about kids*
   - ◇ *Discuss curriculum*
   - ◇ *Work on professional development goals*
   - ◇ *Vent and be around semi-mature adults*
   - ◇ *Work on logistics*
   - ◇ *Share good ideas*
   - ◇ *Talk about team norms and expectations*
   - ◇ *Meet with students and parents or caregivers*
   - ◇ *Work on the weekly homework calendar*
   - ◇ *Update the team website*
   - ◇ *Review student data and progress*

   You'll recognize these reasons as some of the key practices that form the necessary work of a team (see Element 6). Asking and answering this question gives team members an opportunity to restate their priorities for teamwork. You can be sure that the list of reasons will be varied, and it will probably be long. That's okay—this sparks awareness of your beliefs about what needs to happen when you plan together. This awareness will become the basis for the content and structure of all your meetings.

2. **The best logistics and procedures for the meetings.** Ask each other such questions as these. Give everyone a chance to provide suggestions and answers. These will guide your plans for when, where, how, and how long team meetings will proceed.
   - ◇ *How often will we meet? (If not already assigned by the school)*
   - ◇ *Where will we meet?*
   - ◇ *What are the start and end times for our meetings?*
   - ◇ *How will the agenda be established? What will it look like?*
   - ◇ *How shall we begin and end each meeting?*
   - ◇ *Who will lead the meetings? (If a team leader is not assigned)*
   - ◇ *What kind of an agenda will we follow?*
   - ◇ *How will we keep track of what happens in the meetings?*

As you hold these discussions to agree on logistical procedures and reasons for coming together, you form the backbone for what happens when you meet.

Agree on Team Meetings Norms

The commitments you make (above) have to do with logistical details and why the team meets. But team members need to make another kind of promise about what happens at meetings. Great teams set norms—expectations for behaviors and actions that members will follow at all team meetings. Norms provide direction and consistency for team-meeting proceedings and keep teams focused on their tasks.

To help members think about norms, ask such guiding questions as

What do we expect of each other when we meet?
What rules do we follow?
What needs to happen at every meeting?
What should we expect from each team member in terms of participation and engagement?
How can we assure a safe climate for all members?
How do we hold each team member accountable to expectations?

You can discuss and negotiate these norms without making accusations or hurting team members' feelings. Stick to the topics and stay on point. Focus on the question, "What are the acceptable actions during a team meeting?"

Give everyone a chance to name some norms that already exist for the team meetings. Then share suggestions of what might be added, dropped, or changed. Create a list that has general agreement from all members. Be realistic and honest about what norms are needed. Anticipate issues that may arise—and cover these with norms. ***It is truly okay to say that, at no time during the team meeting, is it acceptable to work on your tax return, buy hockey tickets, constantly vent about the same student, or do needle point.***

By the way, since venting about kids is a huge waste of team-meeting time and often leads to no solutions, I heartily encourage all teams to set this norm: Teams get three free vents about any one child. After that—the fourth vent has to be a solution to whatever it is that has generated the complaints.

Great teams review their team norms regularly. This reminds all members of the expectations. It gives teams a chance to make reasoned adjustments. Teams also make sure the lists of norms are posted in the team room, team notebook or Google doc, and conference area.

Here are some examples of team norms. Many of these items below complement and expand on the agreements your team has set for getting along and working together agreeably (see Element 6). But these behaviors and expectations are specific to the team meeting time. When you hold to such expectations as these for team meeting proceedings, you'll get good work done efficiently. And—importantly—you will avoid wasting precious team time.

Your team will create its own norms. They'll choose what is critical for the team's success. Other norms will continue to become evident as you work together. Here are some examples:

We will

- Hold every scheduled meeting.
- Be on time for the meeting.
- Show up at the right location.
- Set a time limit for meetings; and start and end meetings on time.
- Attend every meeting (unless we're not at school that day).
- Review the agenda ahead of time or read it together at the start of the meeting.
- Come prepared. Bring any materials we'll need. Yes, that includes a pen or pencil, paper, laptop. ***(This is what you expect of students, after all!)***
- Leave our own personal work tasks out of the room or away from the team area.
- Stick to the agenda.
- Each actively contributes thoughts and ideas on each topic.
- Let the person talking finish their statement or thought.
- Spend time discussing students' needs (individuals and groups).
- Speak respectfully about students, their family members, and colleagues.
- Keep our comments and discussions bias free.
- Spend time making curriculum and instruction connections.
- Learn something new together.
- Maintain all logs to keep records of communications related to students.

- Respond to team and parent or caregiver emails or texts within 24 hours.
- Share teaching ideas and student data with each other.
- Bring your lists of homework assignments and dates, planned tests or quizzes, and lesson plans.
- Add important happenings to the team calendar.
- Keep good minutes; document decisions and actions from the meeting.
- Honor and support team decisions.
- Take time to encourage each other and laugh together.
- Eat.
- Keep team business confidential.
- Set the time and location for the next team meeting.

Believe it or not, having a set place to meet makes a huge difference. Find a neutral location if possible. Teacher classrooms are oozing with distractions for teachers. If you're meeting in your own classroom, you can always find a project to do. This distracts you and others, and disrupts the meeting. Seek a place that is private and has access to a computer, phone, and a printer or copy machine if possible. I truly understand that, in many of our schools, space is limited, and we are just grateful to have a classroom. Often, a team meeting room is a luxury! Some of the best teaming schools have created a room exclusively for teaming where they display student data and hold family and team meetings. The room is stocked with snacks, coffee, ibuprofen, and Kleenex **(in case someone gets emotional from having a great place to hold their team meetings)**.

Hold Each Other Accountable to the Norms

It's easy to create team norms for a team meeting. The hard part is sticking to the norms and holding each other accountable to them.That's one reason why it is critical that teams design the norms together, rather than following expectations that someone foisted on them. Even when teams have created the norms themselves and agreed to them, they find it hard to establish ways to hold one another to the norms. It can make us uncomfortable to do this. Or, often members will say, "We get along so well that we really don't really need to talk about ways to hold each other accountable."

My response is simple: "It's easier to create ways to hold each other accountable when things are going well versus after you have rolled your eyes twenty times when Mr. Gradebook brings along his papers to grade during team time. Here's why: at that point, you end up creating an accountability method based on that individual's bad behavior. That's not the best way to decide appropriate responses for instances of ignoring expectations."

Great teams respectfully anticipate lapses, addressing issues before they develop. They are proactive—not reactive. This averts situations where a team member pops a gasket and starts yelling at everyone for stuff said or done five years ago.

Here are some ideas for team accountability—in other words, for ways to be respectful to each other and still hold each other to the norms during team time.

1. Create a safe word or phrase (usually something quirky or funny) that anyone can say when the team is off task or not living up to the norms. I like *avocado.* Some teams have used *aardvark, platypus,* or any other weird animal name.
2. Ask how each person wants to be addressed when violating the norms. For example, some teachers might like an email so they process the concerns privately and with a little time. Some like one-on-one responses. Others might want the team to address the issue right away and out in the open. For me, I would hate the one-on-one; I would feel guilty or fear that I let people down. What works for me is something of a joking nature, "Hey Jerkmeyer, (a common name given to me by students when they were angry), "get back on task." I would immediately laugh and apologize and go back to work.

   Yet for some, none of these would be the best approach. I encourage teams to ask each member what method works for them. That way if they get mad when you do hold them accountable, you can remind them that you've used the method they requested. Yes, this is part of making people professionally uncomfortable at times.
3. If things really get ugly, ask the counselor to mediate. Sometimes having another person in the room to listen to all sides and discuss issues helps to de-escalate the situation.
4. Seek administration help. But—this should always be a last resort.

Cohesive learning communities start with the relationships among the adults. The expectations you set for meetings will work well only if the relationships are healthy and valued. Some of these charged situations can be avoided if teams are serious about the commitments they made for getting along (see Element 5) and the norms they set for team-meeting behavior. When things get dicey, remind one another of those. Most clashes are not hard to resolve if adults remember their reasons for teaming and the welfare of the students. Then, hopefully, all members can agree to drop the attitudes and work together in a caring and professional manner.

Set Roles and Responsibilities for Team Members

Once a team has begun to function as a unified group, members must not neglect identifying and distributing the roles and responsibilities necessary to keep it functioning. As you work out (or the team leader assigns) team roles, consider each team member's talents and personal characteristics. Make sure the assignment is suited to a member's strengths.

Take a look at this list of possible roles on a team. Settle on the roles that your team really needs. This is not a set-in-stone decision. Teachers do get bored with the same old dull routines. As time goes on, the roles and responsibilities may be rotated. Also, teams can add, delete, or change roles as needed.

- Team Leader
- Recorder
- Family Contact
- Advisory Liaison
- Newsletter Editor or Team Website Manager
- Communicator with the Essentials (electives) Teachers
- Email Blitzer and Social Media Guru
- Contact for Support Outside the Team (the school guidance office, administrative offices, cafeteria staff, special education department, etc.)
- Snack Master and Social Advisor (Someone who brings treats and snacks. Remember— eating makes a meeting!)

Team roles help a team grow and function. They allow for dividing tasks, giving teachers time to complete some of the work while remaining focused on kids, curriculum, and professional development. See Resource #11, "Team Roles and Responsibilities," on page 200 for a graphic organizer to help you define and assign these.

Create and Follow an Agenda

Agendas give direction to team meetings. They help teams stay on track. They also serve as valuable records of team meetings. Never start a meeting without one! The agenda makes sure we don't waste each other's time and gives us a common goal for each meeting.

Another reason that the agenda is such a powerful tool for team-meeting effectiveness is this: Holding to an agenda minimizes the chances that the varied personal team-meeting styles and needs will pull the meeting off course. For a tongue-in-cheek (but also slightly serious) look at some of what I'll call different "team-meeting personalities," See Resource #12 on page 201. ***I am very much like The Spastic Teacher. I can soar, but I have no landing gears.***

Once you have set priorities for what is important to do at your meetings and detailed how each member will participate and commit to the teaming process, you are ready for regular planning. Decide what components are essential for your team agenda. I've included some sample team-meeting agendas in the Resource section of this book. These can help your team as you developing your own template. See Resources #13, #14, and #15 on pages 202-204.

Be sure that your agenda focuses on kids, curriculum, instruction and assessment, professional development, and some fellowship/logistics/other business. Let me say that again: **Every meeting** should address

Kids (individuals and the group)—discussing their academic progress and needs as well as social, emotional, personal, and behavioral factors; forming and following through on consistent classroom and academic procedures; building relationships; planning advocacy practices; contacting parents or caregivers; or holding student conferences.

Curriculum, instruction, and assessment—sharing teaching plans; coordinating tests, homework, and concepts; connecting curriculum; planning for integrating skills; sharing and evaluating instructional practices; discussing standards; sharing instructional successes.

Professional development—reading or watching and discussing articles, videos, podcasts on educational topics; practicing new instructional techniques; or any other activities that strengthen team practices or teaching practices.

Make time in the agenda for record keeping. Spend the first five minutes reviewing and updating the team calendar. Spend time midway or near the end to add team decisions, planned events, and contacts you've made to your communications log, calendar, and team folder.

Be careful not to let "housekeeping" details take up too much time. Make the agenda fit your team's goals and needs. This should come easily because you began your teamwork together by discussing, "Why do we come together?" (See Elements 5 and 6.)

Keep a copy of your team norms visible during meetings. These will guide you in remembering the components and actions that form the "meat" of the meeting.

When things get hectic, stop and talk about a positive outcome or experience; or each take 15 seconds for each person to say something great that happened for which they are grateful. Make sure you laugh several times during each meeting.

Always wrap up the meeting satisfactorily. Don't just rush out, leaving some or all with a feeling of being unfinished. Exemplary teams recommend that at the end of a meeting, a team should be able to review the agenda and their notes and answer these:

When did the meeting take place?
Who was there?
What was discussed?
What was decided?
Who is responsible for implementation or next steps?
When should implementation be completed?
When will each item be revisited?
What did we add to the team calendar?
What should go on an upcoming agenda?

Be sure that this information is documented on your calendar or other team records. Also, be sure to part ways with warm and kind farewells. Some teams have a chant or a funny phrase.

Know When to Move On

Spending way too much time on kids who are disruptive, disrespectful, non-cooperative—or just unintentionally scattered is something we try to avoid. Yet, in team meetings we spend an inordinate amount of time doing the same—"childrearing" an adult. I firmly believe that if most of the team is on board with a decision or project and working together, then you need to "Move on.org" and not focus on that one obstructive teammate. We have no time to waste on uncooperative adults who want to act in ways that we don't tolerate from the young adolescents we teach.

Please note: I know that dismissing or bypassing the uncooperative or unfocused team member or their opinions is easier said than done. But, yes, at times we need to make each other feel professionally uncomfortable if we are to relate honestly to each other. However, we still have to see that person every day. We need to work well with that person. So, we must have the courage to be direct and kind when telling the person that we must go forward, even with some disagreement. It will help if the team has previously agreed that there are times with a decision when we just fall back on "the majority rules." We need to recognize when it is time to give up trying to force a conversion or epiphany for someone.

Resist the Temptation to Cancel a Team Meeting

Team meeting time is precious—and there is so little of it. No matter how much you have, you can always use more! Yet, invariably, someone seems to come up with a cause to cancel a team meeting. Here are some of the common reasons I hear:

One member of the team is out.
We needed someone to cover a class.
Everyone has too much grading or prep to do.
We're angry at each other.
We're bored with teaming.

I have calls to make.
I have an IEP meeting.

However, great teams have ideas and solutions for avoiding cancelling any meetings. These teams honor team-meeting time as sacred. Remember that your common planning time is absolutely the heart of effective teaming. So, when one or more members just cannot attend the team meeting, find a way to make good use of the time. Perhaps have present members do some of these important tasks instead of the original plan that need the participation of all members.

1. Have everyone on the team call parents or caregivers of five students who are amazing.
2. Send some positive postcards or emails to students or families.
3. Work on your family communication portal.
4. Update your team website or family communication portal.
5. See if the counselor or admin team have any updates they can provide.
6. Email some parents and caregivers or students about missing work.
7. Share some student work with each other.
8. Come up with a reward system for students (or if you have one already—add some new rewards).
9. Decorate the common space.
10. Watch a professional development clip on a topic of interest.
11. Teach each other a new technology strategy.

Faithfully Keep a Team Calendar

Create a team calendar that highlights all major projects, tests or other assessments, due dates, end-of-year reports, progress-report due dates, and any other important team-related important dates. Keep this in the team meeting area or electronically where everyone has easy access. Make the calendar large enough for everyone to see. I am old-school—I like the large desk calendar that so many of our veteran teachers used to use for planning and other important due dates. Maintain or update the calendar on a weekly basis. In fact, every Monday should be Calendar Day at the team meeting.

A great team also posts its team calendar on the team website, in the team notebook, and in the team meeting room. The team sends a monthly calendar home to parents and caregivers about the upcoming events and projects. This helps communicate homework assignments, field trips, and project due dates.

It's a good idea to add teachers' pre-arranged absences to the calendar. This allows the team to plan for any ramifications their absence might have for students. Some of our students do not function well with a guest teacher or substitute teacher. We may know of a specific student who might not be able to (peacefully) **be** in a class with the substitute. Great teams plan for one of the other teachers on the team to take said student into their room for that class period. This proactive move helps decrease discipline referrals and trauma for the student and the guest teacher or substitute.

Here's a sample of what may be on a team calendar. Keep it simple and informative. Team calendars help students, parents and caregivers, and even the most absent-minded teacher.

Calendar Connections

Monday	Tuesday	Wednesday	Thursday	Friday
L.A.: Project Due	Afterschool Make-Up Work Day	Bring-Your-Kid-to-Work Day	Science: Quiz	Math: Assessment
Assembly on Asthma	Social Studies: Poster Due	Math: Fraction Test	Reading: Assessment	Intervention and Enhancement Day
Anti-Bullying Project Due	Band Concert Set 10-Day Learning Goal	Mail 10 Positive Postcards	Mr. Gassman out for Doctor Appointment	Team Awards Celebration
	L.A.: Vocabulary Test	Team Skate Night	Parent Meeting with Ms. McCloud	Next-Week—Academic Success Check

AVOID THESE ACTIONS

In this chapter, you've read about what to do to put Element 7 into action. Here's a quick list of some things **not** to do.

As you **plan and work in team meetings**, steer clear of

1. Starting a meeting without an agenda.
2. Chickening out on holding one another to team norms.
3. Letting a difficult team member take over the meeting.
4. Allowing a team member to get away with behavior you wouldn't accept from students.
5. Grading papers during team meetings.
6. Planning individual class lessons during a team meeting.
7. Texting, surfing, using social media, or taking phone calls during a meeting.
8. Talking about team decisions or issues outside of team meetings.
9. Constantly coming up with excuses to cancel a team meeting.
10. Forgetting to add fun, laughter, and food to the meeting.

ELEMENT 8

Ditch Scattered Expectations

The Successful Middle School: This We Believe Characteristics Crossover

- Educators respect and value young adolescents.
- Health, wellness, and social-emotional competence are supported in curricula, school-wide programs, and related policies.

Great teams are aware of the turmoil caused by a host of varying rules and requirements in the different teachers' classes. They design and commit to using common, consistent procedures and expectations across the team.

WHY THIS ELEMENT IS ESSENTIAL

The entire school community reaps multiple benefits when the teams design common expectations for all classrooms on a team and outline (and teach) regimens and procedures for meeting the expectations.

Here's what I see in schools where this element is done well:

- Teachers are on the same page with everything from sharpening pencils to what happens if the dog ate your homework.
- Students aren't confused. There's a lot less asking, "Where do we put our homework?" or "Whose turn is it to feed the class tarantula?" or "Why can't I leave my backpack in front of your chair?"

- In classrooms, time is not wasted distinguishing expected behaviors and procedures in this class from those in other classes.
- Students are less stressed. They feel secure with the organization and dependability of their daily routines.
- Families don't have to keep track of different rules and expectations from three, four, or more different teachers.
- Administrators have fewer harried questions from bewildered parents or caregivers and fewer visits from students who don't follow rules (sometimes because they are not sure what the rules are or because they repeatedly followed the wrong rule for the wrong classroom).

HOW TO PUT THIS ELEMENT INTO ACTION

I was never an advocate for a list of team expectations. The real reason was simple: I had already created *Mr. Berckemeyer's Alphabet Book*. The book highlighted my list of five or more classroom examples per letter of the alphabet. For example,

A means **always** be on time.

B means **be** polite.

C means keep your **cool** in tense situations (and, that your teacher is **cool**).

D means **desks** are for sitting **at**—not sitting **on.**

It was a never-ending list. I am sure that the alphabet book was the sole reason students came to sixth grade. I know each one went home at the end of the school day and memorized all 55,000 expectations I had designed for them. ***I used this alphabet book for several years.***

I will never forget when my teammates came to me one year and said, "Jack, we need to be more consistent."

I answered, "Yes, you do." ***Another phrase I learned to regret.*** I told them I already had my list of expectations and felt that it worked for me.

Well, not six days after the conversation with my teammates, I noticed a young man from my 6th-grade class go into the restroom and then walk right back out.

I thought to myself, "I know he is not flushing the toilet, and he is certainly not washing his hands."

So being a good teacher, I told him that he needed to flush the toilet and wash his hands when he used the restroom. He replied that he didn't go into the bathroom to actually **use** the restroom. He said, "In your alphabet book, you said we had to go to the bathroom before we came to your class." Once again, I was duped by an 11-year-old.

I started to realize that my list was for me—not for my team, and not for the benefit of my students. So, I walked into my team meeting and informed my teammates that I was ready to create a list of team expectations for all our students. The concern that I had was making sure that the team keep it simple. I requested that we begin by giving students no more than five to seven items to learn at a time. (We can always add others later, I argued.) ***We are talking about young adolescents. My alphabet book had shown me that the list of expectations could be too long.***

Oh, and one more stipulation—I just needed the list to address my personal pet peeve. To some of you, this one might seem trivial or even crazy, but to me it's a big deal: I am not a fan of kids sitting on their desktops. It drives me crazy, and I think it rude. The hard part was trying to convince my teammates that this was a legitimate issue. After exerting a vast amount of time and energy with me demonstrating real-life examples of the perils of sitting on top of a desk, my teammates agreed not to allow kids to sit on their desks. I know they thought I was a freak, but victory was mine! We did go on to agree to some other common procedures, and consistency within our team was enhanced.

Identify and Analyze Current Expectations

The global pandemic, with its interruptions to regular in-school learning, left our students with a lack of consistency—the one thing they craved from us that we were not able to provide for several months. Many educators have noticed that all age groups suffered from being outside the safe structure of school. In many cases, students came back lacking social graces, common courtesy, and respect ***(just as their teachers came back lacking anything in their wardrobes but sweats***

and tube socks with holes in them). The kids had forgotten how to "do" school. Educators across the world said, "I can't believe they don't know how to..." Such simple things as opening a locker, walking on the right side of the hall, and knowing how to hold a pencil were left behind due to virtual teaching and, in some cases, unstructured home life.

Consistent procedures across the classrooms of one team have always been a good idea. Students and teachers have forever needed a dependable environment. Teaming provides the kind of structure and security that helps students learn and function well. It's always been the case (even pre-pandemic) that confusion and chaos abound when each teacher has different procedures for such things as arrival and dismissal, heading for the bathroom, turning in assignments, and late work.

Now, more than ever, we teachers on teams must have tough conversations about what our students really need from us. We need to stop fighting with each other about "things that are not my battle" or such matters as "I don't mind them wearing earbuds even though you might." In these cases, **all** must mean **all**. We all must fight the consistency fights; we all must hold each other accountable and be one united front. What solves this issue? Consistent teaming!

Have you ever taken time as a team to write down all the classroom expectations for all the different teachers that a middle school student on your team faces during the day? You might think that it's not all that different from one class to another. But you won't be sure about these unless you put them under a microscope!

Before creating common team expectations, identify all existing procedures and check for consistencies and inconsistencies.

1. Define what you mean by procedures, rules, and expectations. You might come up with descriptions such as:

   A protocol (or rule) is a guide or rule for conduct or action in a certain situation.

   A procedure (or routine) is a series of detailed actions to follow to accomplish a specific task or process.

   An expectation is an assumption or intention that the protocols or procedures will be followed.

2. Do the following simple exercise to get a feel for the variety of expectations that already exist in your classes. Choose just a couple areas of routines or procedures. Have each team member describe their rules for that area.

   For example, here's a result when one team charted each teacher's expectation related to one small matter of academic work:

Heading on Papers

Teacher	Class	Expectation
Ms. Rubinowitz	**Language Arts**	Name, date, and period Right-hand corner
Mr. Berckemeyer	**Science**	Name, date, and period Right-hand corner
Ms. Trumbo	**Special Ed**	First name only
Mr. Gassman	**Social Studies**	First and last name

Here's another example. This shows the varied expectations related to one management procedure.

In-Class Cell Phone Use

Teacher	Class	Expectation
Ms. Rubinowitz	**Language Arts**	Phones are collected at the beginning of the period and returned when students leave.
Mr. Berckemeyer	**Science**	The phone must either be in their backpack or clear pouch that is in the front of the room (looks like a shoe holder).
Ms. Trumbo	**Special Ed**	Cell phones are never to be seen or heard.
Mr. Gassman	**Social Studies**	Cell phones must be turned off during tests only.

By the way, were you counting? That's seven different expectations for just two procedures.

3. Discuss the outcomes of the exercise. Using these examples, see if your team could come to a common expectation in each of these two areas.
4. Next, expand this exercise. Together, brainstorm a list of all or many of the protocols and procedures you already have in your classrooms. Here are some samples of expectations that might be on your list:

   Management Procedures. These apply to routines and rules of classroom life. Some examples are:

   - Schedule for the day or week
   - Tardy policies
   - Excused or unexcused absences
   - Discipline policies
   - Cell phone use
   - How students identify names and pronouns
   - Hoodies or other dress code matters
   - Earning bonus points for academic work
   - What to do when arriving at class
   - What to do when class is over
   - Moving about in the classroom
   - Getting and using hall passes
   - Leaving the room
   - Sharpening pencils
   - Putting stuff in the trash
   - Organization of supplies
   - Borrowing supplies
   - Internet use
   - Logistics of small group work
   - Student role in governance
   - Assemblies
   - Guest speakers
   - Field trips

- ◇ Rewards and recognitions

Instructional Procedures. These are routines or expectations related to academic learning. Some examples are:

- ◇ Getting and keeping track of assignments
- ◇ Organizing work
- ◇ Learning together in small groups
- ◇ Handing in homework
- ◇ Headings on papers
- ◇ Late work
- ◇ Taking tests or quizzes
- ◇ Media use
- ◇ Makeup work or do-overs
- ◇ Extra credit
- ◇ Grading
- ◇ Feedback on work
- ◇ Student conferences
- ◇ Proficiency (or deficiency) reports
- ◇ Special projects

5. Use a spreadsheet or table such as Resource #16, "Examining Our Team's Current Expectations," on page 205. This gives you a place to note expectations that each team member now holds on each rule or procedure.

Create Your Team's Consistent Expectations

Here are some steps to design consistent expectations across the team.

1. Analyze your team's list or spreadsheet of existing procedures. Together, look for places where you already have consist expectations. Commit to keeping up the consistency for these items!
2. Look for other items where your current practices are close. See what you can tweak to align those across the team.
3. It will be easiest to keep a record of policies if you group them into categories. Agree on general categories for identifying expectations and

procedures. These could be such areas as those noted above, or any number of others.

4. For each category, write the consistent protocols or procedures that you decide to create. For a template of how to write your chosen consistent expectations see Resource #17, "Our Team Protocols," on page 206.
5. Then get to work! Look for ways to compromise and become more consistent for the benefit of the students.
6. Start with the easy protocols, such as putting the heading on a paper. You want to experience success. Take your time on each one to determine the expectations and the consequences for the students.
7. I also suggest that you try to tackle first those matters that are foundational to smooth operations in the classroom—particularly the simpler things for which students will need to establish good habits from the beginning. This might be such routines as coming and going from class, getting hall passes, keeping track of assignments, or asking questions.
8. Work up to the more difficult items such as grading policies and late work. The reality is that everyone on the team will likely have different expectations for if, how, and when they will accept assignments that are not turned in on time. You could have one teacher who deems work to be late minutes after it is first collected from the class and another who gives kids until the end of the quarter. And then there's the team member who says, "As long as it is handed in by the end of the universe, I will give them credit!" Such policies as these will take more discussion and compromise.

Put the Consistent Procedures into Practice

Make a plan for putting your expectations into practice. Your lists of consistency items may be long, so communicating them to students and building them into habits will take thought and time. Here's some advice on that:

- **Do not** introduce the students to all your newly formed consistent expectations all at once! Start with a few (three to five) at a time. This venture is about quality, not quantity. You'll benefit far more from a few taught and practiced well than 50 all jumbled together and forgotten.

- **Teach** each expectation to the students. Show (don't just tell) them the specifics of the expectation. Demonstrate it. (For example, walk across the classroom and sharpen a pencil in a non-disruptive, efficient way—with no intentionally spastic movements.) Enlist students to role-play and demonstrate the procedures. Or they can make a simple game out of practicing a procedure. They'll pick up the process much more quickly from actually doing it.
- Don't assume that one exposure sets the process in stone. They'll need ongoing demonstrations and affirmations until an expectation becomes a habit. Review and refresh these often. This does not mean that you have to stop and give a half-hour lesson on each of these. You can strengthen and refresh them in small doses as a normal part of the daily routines.
- Follow the expectations yourself. When you do not allow use of cell phones, but you're on yours during class—you send a very mixed message to your students. Stop using the excuse that you are an adult and can do anything you want.
- Present all these expectations to students as guidelines for a successful classroom—rather than as a list of rules you can't break. Kids are more likely to follow them when they understand the reasons.
- Where possible, ask for their help in setting a procedure. Or, you might alter a procedure when students have better suggestions. The greater their involvement in each procedure, the more likely they are to own and follow it.
- Find time for students to ask questions and discuss expectations. Invite their input. They can give this on surveys, with individual notes, or in small-group discussions. Or they might anonymously contribute topics or questions for discussion.
- There are expectations that go beyond classroom procedures. Invite students to respond to expectations for life together in the classrooms and on the team. Encourage them to watch for bias or discrimination items that need to be addressed on the team (sexism, racism, ablism, classism, gender

discrimination, religious intolerance, body shaming, etc.). Students notice incidents and innuendos that teachers often miss. Find safe ways for them to share and discuss what they see.

Keep Up the Consistency

The hard part will be remaining consistent within the team. The students will live up to the expectations; the people who will not live up to the expectations will be you and your teammates. For example, you might have an expectation about not sitting on the tops of desks, as I do. Everyone on your team might agree to that expectation. However, during passing period you might walk by a teammate's room and see a student sitting on the desktop. ***Or maybe you will even see the teacher sitting on a desk!*** Observing this lack of respect for the expectation causes several emotions from a fellow teammate. First anger, then spite, and, ultimately, the desire for revenge. So, you either badmouth Mr. Toombs behind his back or ignore him for a period of time.

The next thing that happens in this case is that students then come into your room and proceed to sit on the desktops. You say, "Get off the desk!"

They say, "Mr. Toombs lets us!"

You say, "Do I look like Mr. Toombs? Am I wearing a hairpiece and an ugly beard?"

This is a case of educational sabotage ***(and not a good idea, of course)***.

During team-meeting time, members need to remind each other of the expectations and ask each other, "Why are we not supporting the list of expectations?"

Here's the deal: As teachers, we confront parents and caregivers, kids, or our administrators as long as two other people come with us! The hardest person to confront is a fellow teacher. Many times, instead of talking through and resolving the situation, we just remain bitter and angry. I know teachers who have carried a grudge about another teacher for years. Let it go! There are so many people against us as educators. **Let's not turn on each other.**

We have to learn that good teaming involves some dialogue and some conflict. It takes work and good communication to remain consistent. It also takes effort and the ability to be honest with each other. If we remain consistent with each other, it will help us stay on the same page. We know that middle school students want some consistency in their turbulent lives. We can provide that by creating basic policies and procedures that we all hold to. This may even help decrease classroom interruptions and the need to repeat everything.

Remember—the most inconsistent person in the room is almost always the teacher!

AVOID THESE ACTIONS

In this chapter, you've read about what to do to put Element 8 into action. Here's a quick list of some things **not** to do.

As you work to **ditch scattered expectations and design and follow through on consistent protocols and procedures,** steer clear of

1. Giving kids all 40 (or 100) expectations at the same time.
2. Overlooking the importance of involving students in the process of identifying and discussing items for consistency.
3. Neglecting to reinforce the expectations regularly throughout the year.
4. Getting lax about holding students and team members to the expectations.
5. Failing to keep a clear (and written) list of protocols and procedures.
6. Forgetting to let parents and caregivers know about the expectations.
7. Presenting skills of being a good human being as your consistent rules. Such things as being polite, kind, and respectful; raising your hand; and not talking when someone else is talking are already well-stated, consistent expectations.

ELEMENT 9

Spark Team Identity and Unity with Students

The Successful Middle School: This We Believe Characteristics Crossover

- Educators respect and value young adolescents.
- The school environment is welcoming, inclusive, and affirming for all.

Great teams actively engage students in developing and maintaining the cohesion and unique identity of the team. They plan frequent moments and events to build a dynamic team spirit.

WHY THIS ELEMENT IS ESSENTIAL

All members of the school community reap significant benefits when teachers and students together value and inspire ongoing habits to BE a team and grow team connections.

Here's what I see in schools where this element is done well:

- Teachers have fun. They enjoy the spirit of harmony and solidarity developing among students on the team.
- Students are proud and excited to be part of **their** team. They are more likely to want to come to school. Attendance rates increase.
- Teams have unique names and personalities. Students enjoy spreading the word about their team identity through logos, T-shirts, flags, etc.

- Students actively participate in the workings of the team. They feel free to contribute suggestions and ideas in their team. Student voice and choice blossom.
- Students have fun. The unity and identity activities connect students with one another as well as with the team.
- Team unity among the adults on the team ignites student unity, and vice versa.
- Leaders feel the energy fueled by the rise in team spirit of teams across the school.
- Parents and caregivers are glad to see their children participating in team events, and are proud to witness their individual child's recognition for their unique gifts and accomplishments.

HOW TO PUT THIS ELEMENT INTO ACTION

You just can't overestimate the value of taking time to build a unified team (with all the adults and students together). These efforts help students belong, learn better, and feel like vital parts of the learning community. A solid experience of unity comes from empowering students to take part in shaping their team's identity and spirit. It's further enhanced when we engage them in creating the classroom culture and when we trust them with tasks and responsibilities.

Discuss the Teaming Concept with Students

Students need to know what an interdisciplinary team (or whatever kind of team you're implementing) is, why they are on a team, and how the teaming process may differ from the way their days were previously structured. In addition, they need to begin developing a sense of **THEIR** team—what is unique about it, what its purpose is. Team unity is about more than the warm fuzziness of being together and having a place to belong. Students need to know how teaming helps them be successful academically and as people. Here are some ways the teachers can boost students' understanding of teaming:

1. Ask for students' ideas. What do they know about teaming? What have they heard? What do they think might be some benefits of having teams?

2. Tell students what you, the teachers, love about teaming and why you want to be on a team. Share what you believe to be the core values and proven benefits of teaming.
3. Share what's unique about this team. Even if you haven't gotten to know the students yet, give them a taste of how they are not exactly like any other team.
4. If the teachers have created a team philosophy or vision, share this with students. Let them respond to it or ask questions about it.
5. Students can create their own statement about who or what their team is or what they want it to be. This can be in the form of belief statements, a mission, a philosophy, a description, or a slogan. This is best done after a few weeks together, when they've had a chance to pick up on the developing team personality—and when they've gotten some sense of what they might hope to accomplish as a team. They can publicize this on a poster, video, website announcement, or other way of their choice.
6. Discuss with students the reasons for common expectations and protocols across the team for classrooms and hallways. Explain why the team has common grading practices, late work policies, and common reward systems.

Name the Team

To encourage team unity and a distinct identity, most schools come up with team names. It is always interesting to ask teachers why they have team names. Many teachers just say it is something the school has been doing for years. Some are not sure why it happens.

Unfortunately, sometimes teachers have more ownership of their team's name than the students do. I once asked a teacher why her team was called *The Jaguars*, and she simply stated that it was because she already had a bunch of laminated posters of jaguars. **Now, we DO know how much teachers love to laminate things for the classroom. I think there are some who would laminate the class gerbil if they could. But a set of laminated posters is not a good reason for a particular choice of a team name.**

It's a common mistake to forget about asking students for their input. Yes, it takes time and energy to consult students about a team name, but student ownership comes with student input. Student voice and choice are key, research-backed attributes of a high-performing middle grades school, as emphasized in AMLE's *The Successful Middle School: This We Believe.*[11] I'll admit that in the past, I too had little emotional attachment to the naming of teams. Now, I've come to see that it is critical to the success of teaming.

Here are some simple ways to involve students in the process:

- Near the beginning of the year, let students know that there will be a contest for choosing the team's name from all the ideas submitted. You might offer a reward for the student or students who come up with the winning name.
- Teachers may want to set a common theme, limiting ideas to that category. For example, in one school all eighth grade teams have space-related names.
- Invite students to contribute ideas during advisory time or home base.
- Eliminate inappropriate and repetitive ideas from the list. If the list is still very long, you might hold an initial student vote to hone it down to the top ten. Or a task force can narrow down the ideas and present them to the entire team. ***Remember that the teachers have the right of refusal when it comes to the team name. Kids can be sneaky; and we teachers might be way out of the loop about some of the current lingo and pop culture phrases. Students could give you an acronym for a team name like Caring, Responsible, Appreciative, People (C.R.A.P.).***
- Once the vote is taken and the winner is chosen, students can create a logo, design a team flag or banner, or engage in other activities that create a recognizable identity for the team. Some schools retire old team names and hang the banners in the gym. This is similar to traditions for winning sports team banners or players' numbers on jerseys; once the name is on a banner, another team can never use it.

Make Team-Unity Activities Part of Your Routine

A sense of "who we are," of "we are all in this together," and of "we can do great things together" flourishes when you plan team-wide activities. Team spirit soars as well. Make a list of possibilities for things the team can create, do, and contribute together to solidify team identity and deepen team unity. Ask kids to contribute to the list; better yet—ask them to make the list. This is a great chance for them to lend their voices and make choices. Trust me, they'll have creative and thoughtful suggestions. Be sure to incorporate their ideas before finalizing your plans. Here are some ideas to get you started. These are for the whole team to do together—students and teachers included. ***Yes, teachers—don't ever stand on the side and watch team-spirit activities!***

Things to Create Together

- Team motto or creed
- Team logo, symbol, or crest
- Team flag, colors, or banner
- T-shirt, hat, or socks
- Team signal, handshake, or no-touch "handshake"
- Team song, dance, cheer, or mime
- Mural—everybody contributes something related to the team
- An "Orientation Guide to Our Team" for new students who join the team
- Team scrapbook or calendar

Things to Do Together

- Prepare a student survey to get feedback on team spirit, unity, or general climate.
- Decorate the classroom door.
- Hold team field trips, games, tournaments, bulletin boards, or after-school activities.
- Plan an academic fair where kids teach something to others or feature projects.

Ways to Foster an Attitude of Caring within the Team

- Collect food, clothing, or toys for a community organization.
- Collect recyclables and donate the cash to a community organization.
- Gather items for a nearby animal shelter.
- Help the teachers rearrange or redecorate the classroom.
- Volunteer to clean up the playground or cafeteria.
- Join community efforts for clean-up days or fundraising.
- Help other grade-level classes with projects.

Laugh Together

A good laugh is great for bonding! There is nothing more powerful than a classroom or team with teachers who are joyful and each have a good sense of humor. Yes, humor is serious business. It has been shown that laughter improves your immune system and your heart function, helps you recover better from injuries and illness, and that everyone should laugh many times a day. **By the way, children laugh an average of 400 times a day. By the time they get to be adults, that reduces to fewer than 20 times a day. And I bet I know some educators who probably haven't laughed yet this week.**

Humor can defuse stress and tension and decrease classroom discipline problems. It dissipates bad moods and increases enthusiasm. It grabs the attention of distracted students and holds their interest in content. It helps students (and teachers) relax, boosts morale, and ignites togetherness. **This isn't just what research tells; I've witnessed this hundreds of times. You probably have, as well.** Don't forget to make fun and laughter a regular part of team life. Students will love being on the team, and so will teachers.

A few tips:

- You don't have to be a stand-up comedian to add laughter to the mix. Just relaxing and enjoying yourself and your students can lead to normal humor. It might be something as simple as finding funny memes, showing short, funny (appropriate) YouTube clips, telling a dad joke of the day, or showing students your high school prom picture.
- Really, anybody can share a funny story or video, wear a costume or disguise, act out an important concept (osmosis) or process (making a timeline by hopping along an imaginary line), break into a crazy song or dance, mix up a sentence, throw in a malapropism, or teach a key concept with a silly poem.
- As a teacher, laugh at yourself. Teammates, laugh at each other (kindly). Show students that you don't take yourselves too seriously.
- Ask teammates to remind you when you haven't laughed enough or inspired students to laugh often.

- Humor can be harmful. Never use it to mock or disparage anyone. Don't single out a certain student. Don't use it in ways that would give students the idea that you're making fun of their names, work, answers, opinions, or behavior.
- Stay away from sarcasm. Too often, it contains a hidden or outright insult.
- The teacher sets the tone for how humor is used. Students will take their cues from you. As a team, commit to healthy, uplifting, wholesome humor.
- Appreciate and enjoy the pre-adolescent or adolescent humor when possible. If you teach at the middle- or high-school levels, you know the difference between those occasions when it's okay to laugh and when it is not. Don't take students' humor personally. And don't ever laugh if it is rude or demeaning. Address those instances when they occur.

Humor belongs in every classroom. Let it refresh and vitalize your team's classrooms, team meetings, and all-team gatherings.

Create Team Rewards

Teams are constantly looking for ways to motivate students. There is an interesting debate about how often and how much we should reward students. In her book, *Fall Down 7 Times, Get Up 8*, Dr. Debbie Silver asserts that there is no single right answer to how to reward students. She suggests that, in most cases, less is more. I think Debbie is correct: It is not about the quantity; it is about the quality of team rewards. For a thorough, balanced approach to the topic of rewards, I recommend that you read Debbie's Chapter 6, titled, "What Do I Get for Doing It?"[12] **By the way, do read and discus Debbie's chapter as a team. This will offer you a great professional development opportunity!**

We know that young adolescents crave adult interactions. Maybe team lunches with the teachers, or other one-on-one time with a teacher are enough for a student reward. In many cases, young adolescents are seeking someone just to listen to them. It is not about candy and extra bonus points. **Let's be honest: If a student likes you and likes the class, they will work for dirt in a Dixie cup.**

I encourage teams to look closely at how rewards such as stars, stickers, and bonus points impact a student's work ethic. I do believe in praise for students. I believe that simple things like a warm smile and a slight thumbs-up do help. But do rewards improve behavior? Do they increase achievement and comprehension? True comprehension, academic success, and real improvements in social skills come from hard work, dedication, practice, and time. And such intrinsic rewards as self-satisfaction, pride in oneself, and self-esteem are longer-lasting than pizzas or trinkets. ***Maybe a team can look for ways to honor those characteristics, instead.***

However, extrinsic rewards can be fun and motivating. Scientists have found that receiving compliments and recognition causes the release of dopamine in the brain, giving a boost to motivation.[13] Schools, teachers, and kids often love rewards. We just have to be thoughtful in considering what kinds of rewards further the goals we are trying to reach and the behaviors or skills we are trying to strengthen. Be sure to keep track of the rewards you give and the students to whom they were given (and the dates). ***More data for your team notebooks or team folders. See Element 14 for record-keeping and documentation advice.***

Kinds of Rewards

School-level rewards. Schools offer a variety of rewards. We have the student-of-the-month or week or student-of-the-moment. Most schools have attendance rewards, certificates for high grades, or awards based on school-wide attributes such as courage, honesty, humor, or willingness to help others. Teams might not have input into these awards other than submitting student names. For many of the buildings, rewards have been established for years. In many cases these have not been reconsidered or changed (perhaps ever).

> *Advice:* I would have a team of students and teachers work together on possible building-wide rewards. Individual teams in the school can send representatives to this committee. It might be time to change up the honor roll and perfect attendance awards.

Classroom rewards. There are also rewards devised and given by individual teachers for students in their classrooms. Many teachers have established rewards for classroom procedures, completion of work, manners, and behavior. For some, this helps manage a classroom and allows for the teacher to honor good deeds and behaviors. One of the hardest transitions for a team is, often, convincing an individual teacher to give up their classroom rewards and embrace a team-wide approach.

Advice: Teammates should look for rewards that are consistent among the team, replacing any individual classroom awards. This move helps with consistency and might increase the value of the rewards.

Team-wide rewards. Great teams develop rewards systems that all team members embrace, implement, and support. Having the team create rewards helps students live up to common expectations, procedures, and policies. Teams also regularly reflect on their reward systems. I would encourage that the team, along with a focus group of students, re-evaluate their reward systems each semester. Student input is key; after all, they are the ones earning the rewards.

Advice: One of the best rewards systems I have seen has this feature: The student who earns the reward nominates another student for the award. Please note that the adults would have right of refusal on the student's suggestions. For example, "I nominate Abernathy for the organization award." Yet, teachers on the team know that Abernathy has eight weeks of work in her binder and still can't remember her locker combination (even though it's the locker bulging at the hinges with junk, emanating strange fumes). Students need to know the criteria when picking other students.

Five Musts for Creating Team Rewards

1. Stop establishing rewards for the entire year or semester. Rewards should apply to a shorter term and be easy to implement. Depending on your specific students, the goal could be for a month, week, day, or one hour. For some students, it could be a reward every three minutes.
2. Have a visual aid that allows students to see progress. Use a dry-erase board or create a thermometer such as those you see for fundraisers. Students

need to be able to witness how they are doing and make updates to the visual after each day or class period.

3. Arrange for students to select rewards, and make the rewards tangible. Our students who constantly play video games work for intangible rewards. The computer game does not give out stickers, snacks, or socialization time. The game-players are basically seeking rewards that just get them to a higher level or more points. They are missing and craving rewards they can touch, feel, smell, (maybe eat), and hold.
4. Rewards can also be events such as dance contests or the team singing a song. I must admit, there are some cool dances on TikTok. If you are using food rewards, they can be theme-based. For example: a Snickers for a good sense of humor, Mounds bar for hurdling over an obstacle, or a Jolly Rancher for being happy and friendly. **Please refrain from using Dum Dums and anything with a "dud" in the title. But Smarties are a nice option for doing well on an assignment.**
5. Kids love teacher versus student competitions as rewards. I have lost many battles with students and ended up singing "'I'm a Little Teapot" in front of the class.
   Advice: When designing awards or special events, try not to worry too much about the students who might be in a non-team class during that time. There are ways to deal with situations. I see some team members shutting down great ideas because seven kids will miss out. I am sure there will be opportunities to involve those students in other ways.

Celebrate Together

Great teams look for unique ways to celebrate students on the team. Students will feel connected with the team that commemorates team accomplishments and finds ways to recognize and honor them. And when we involve students in the planning and operation of these events, we offer another way to boost student participation, voice, choice, decision-making, and cooperation. Such team celebrations are a time to recognize individual attainments as well as team milestones.

One way to celebrate daily is to find an area at the school (a hallway or other area that has a large bulletin board or plenty of wall space). Use this to display student writing, artwork, and team pictures. You don't always have to hold an event to show off team unity and accomplishments!

In addition, teams plan regular events where the whole group gets together to celebrate—as often as monthly. You'll have to find a space large enough for your whole team, and will likely need to reserve it ahead of time. Some of your celebrations can be on the playground, soccer field, or school track.

When you prepare for a celebration,

- Plan to celebrate individual accomplishments as well as all-team milestones or achievements.
- Find out what students want. Get their suggestions about what to celebrate and about what makes for a celebratory atmosphere. They will have creative ideas for interesting and meaningful awards, and for places and ways to celebrate.
- Decide who will coordinate and "run" the event. Use students in these roles as much as possible.
- Be sure to include some out-of-the-ordinary awards and even some funny or wacky awards.
- Make each award something tangible, meaningful, and memorable—not just a certificate.

Here are some occasions and accomplishments to celebrate and some ways to do so:

Team celebratory events or team honors

- A tailgate party for your students before a home basketball or football game
- Everyone met an objective or standard celebration
- End-of-testing celebration
- A giving celebration (Students who give to someone else in some way can attend a party or celebration.)
- Celebration for a month of no tardies on the team
- Celebration for everyone surviving a tough month or finishing a huge project
- Team dance, ice cream party, or picnic
- Math night, poetry slam, or literacy festival

Individual recognition (or sometimes a few individuals at once)

- Birthdays—all the birthdays for the month, perhaps
- Celebrations for outstanding work on a class project
- Outside-of-school accomplishments such as 4H **("Way to go, Angela! Your goat won Best-in-Show!")**
- Presentations by school clubs (sports, debate, robotics, etc.)
- Group dance or theater presentations
- Grade-changing award—honoring students who have increased their grades for the quarter
- Student who has the best smelling deodorant ***(I am checking to see if you are paying attention.)***
- On-time-and-ready award—given to students regularly who come prepared for class
- "Hey, that was nice" award—given when students do nice things for each other
- Thought-provoking award—given when a student says something that is profound and interesting
- Stumped-the-teacher award—given when a student comes up with an answer that even the teacher did not predict
- Outstanding artist or cartoonist award (or rapper, dancer, mime, etc.)
- Helping-those-who-help-others award
- Technology-support award—given to students who help other kids with computer or technology issues
- Top-of-the-line award—for students who are always polite and kind
- Great-humor award—given to the student(s) who keep us joyful
- Congeniality award—for student(s) who are especially friendly and agreeable

Hold Regular All-Team Meetings

Now and then, the whole team needs to get together to take care of matters of team business, team learning, and team life—or just to celebrate. All-team meetings can help to keep students focused on the team as a learning community. They boost team unity and increase a sense of belonging and togetherness. Kids learn more about each other, hear each other's ideas and opinions, and have fun. These are fantastic settings for increasing team unity. They also offer wonderful opportunities for strengthening skills of self-expression, listening, reasoning, problem-solving, decision-making, and cooperation.

Some advice for all-team meetings:

- Have a clear leader. At the beginning, this would be a teacher. But after some experience with all-team meetings, a student can lead the meeting. Or a few students can each lead parts of the meeting.
- Have an agenda. Identify a reasonable number of components for the allotted time. Teachers prepare the early agendas. But after some experience with the meetings, students can contribute to the agendas or even create them.
- Include items such as these in a team meeting:
    - ◇ Succinct team announcements
    - ◇ An enticing preview of upcoming team-wide curriculum
    - ◇ Showcase of individual or team achievements, improvements, kindnesses
    - ◇ Discussions, responses, and ideas related to team procedure
    - ◇ Discussion and resolution of a team issue
    - ◇ Student input on classroom procedures, events, projects, homework, schedules, or assignments
    - ◇ Fun community-building activities, such as: skits, solving a problem or puzzle together.
    - ◇ Opportunity for students to ask questions or make comments
    - ◇ Sharing gratitude comments

      Note: Some of the above items can be pre-recorded (videotaped) ahead of time for use at an all-team gathering.
- Follow the agenda.
- End with team "virtual" hug or handshake, or chant your team motto.

AVOID THESE ACTIONS

In this chapter, you've read about what to do to put Element 9 into action. Here's a quick list of some things **not** to do.

As you **work to ignite and nurture team identity and unity**, steer clear of

1. Forgetting ample, regular doses of humor and fun for the team.

2. Leaving students out of any of the processes and steps for this element.
3. Neglecting to include parents and caregivers in celebrations, where possible.
4. Giving too many rewards that are purely extrinsic and not meaningful or memorable.
5. Undervaluing the long-term benefits (to teachers and students) for academic success, relationships, social and emotional skills, healthy climate, and school connection that result from a solid focus on team identity and unity.

ELEMENT 10

Discipline with Consistency

The Successful Middle School: This We Believe
Characteristics Crossover

- Educators respect and value young adolescents.
- School safety is addressed proactively, justly, and thoughtfully.
- The school engages families as valued partners.
- Policies and practices are student-centered, unbiased, and fairly implemented.

G**reat teams** create and follow a common cross-team discipline process. They apply this consistently to all matters of discipline that can possibly be handled by the team.

WHY THIS ELEMENT IS ESSENTIAL

All members of the school community reap important benefits when the teams handle most misbehaviors and conduct violations whenever possible.

Here's what I see in schools where this element is done well:

- Teachers on the team are less stressed about discipline. They have a spirit of unity and mutual support in following the same guidelines. There is no ambiguity about what to do when a problem arises.
- Teachers know which kinds of problems to handle and which kinds to refer elsewhere. They have pre-determined responses and interventions to specific discipline issues.

- Teachers have classroom management matters under control. Classroom life is smoother. Everyone is on the same page and the students know it.
- No matter which teacher is in charge, students are clear on expectations and the discipline process. They can't say, "But Mr. So-and-So doesn't care if we .... "
- Parents and caregivers are informed about the team discipline process. They have it in writing. There is less confusion about what is expected for their children. When a problem arises with a student, the parents and caregivers know how it will be handled. Families are able communicate with a united set of teachers instead of three or more individuals, each of whom may have different rules.
- Administrators deal with larger issues and not the minor disruptions that the team can handle through a meeting with the student or a phone call. They are able to concentrate on the tougher issues that have consequences of school suspensions, expulsions, or legal violations.

HOW TO PUT THIS ELEMENT INTO ACTION

"The best people to deal with discipline are the classroom teachers and teams—not the administrator!" This is a Jack Berckemeyer quote, something that I have been saying for years. Yet, I notice again and again that teams and teachers neglect the responsibility of dealing with minor discipline issues. To handle issues of behavior in the way that is healthiest for the students—and also the most effective—teams must face their reluctance about discipline matters and phone calls to parents or caregivers (either negative or positive calls). They must form workable processes for taking care of minor cases of bad behavior, uncooperative attitudes, or rule-breaking.

Examine the Team's Current Approach to Discipline

As a first step to forming (or polishing) positive and consistent process for discipline, a great team will have an honest discussion about what's going on right now (or in your past years as a team). Sit together and ask yourselves such questions as these:

How do we handle situations in which students act rudely, have troubles with self-control, violate codes of conduct, or ignore expectations?
How consistent are we within the team as to responses and consequences?
Does every teacher equally hold students to whatever expectations have been put forth in their classroom?
How often do we evade the problem and send it on to someone outside the team?
Should we explore de-escalation and restorative practices?
How do we increase our knowledge of our student population?
How do we include more student voice in discipline?
What trauma-informed discipline responses do we use?

Notice common answers the teammates shared. Take time to further explore any answers that needed clarification.

As I said, far too many discipline issues are passed off to an administrator or some other school leader. Here are some of the reasons team members have gotten into this habit:

- Belief that it's just easier to ask a kid to leave the class and have someone else deal with the behavior.
- Lack of training on how to handle minor issues.
- Worry about parent or caregiver reactions to consequences for the student.
- Lack of consistency among teachers' responses to an issue.
- Teacher attitude of "It's not my battle," so they let things go.
- Absence of policies and procedures in place for a team to do their own discipline.
- Lack of support to teams and teachers who try to deal with some tough problems.
- Lack of willingness by some or all teachers on the team to try a team plan.
- Lack of training on de-escalation approaches and restorative practices.

Commit to Handling Most Discipline Issues Within the Team

We are often too hasty to ask administrators to step in and help us deal with classroom management issues—when most issues are manageable within the team. Here are some reasons **not to send the student to the administrator**:

1. The administrator often has a less personal or meaningful relationship with the student. Unlike the teacher or other team members, they don't know the student's history, personality, and needs.
2. Neither does the administrator have all the details about what happened—or the background on the specific incident. The teacher was there when it was brewing and when it happened, and witnessed the fallout. ***All the administrator has is a referral written in haste and anger by the classroom teacher. An administrator can tell how mad the teacher is by the number of exclamation points and (if it is handwritten) by the torn spot where some words are underlined nine times.***
3. When you (a teacher) send a student to the principal, your influence and authority are weakened. Kids (not just the student in question) get the message that you can't handle them or the problems—that the teacher or teachers on the team are not in control. They respect the teachers less. (Understand that handling a problem within the team doesn't mean that you always have to keep the student in the classroom. You might need to send the student elsewhere for the remainder of the class without turning the problem over to the principal. And as soon as possible, you'd bring them back to discuss their actions during a team meeting.)
4. The more you send kids off to the principal, the more difficult classroom management becomes. It's disruptive to your classroom work time. The other students lose ability to focus on anything besides what's happening to that one student, even after the kid leaves. When the student returns, other students are even less engaged—probably for the rest of the period! And worse, the student with the problem will likely get bolder in their misbehavior.
5. And guess what? You don't get to let the principal keep the kid. Administrators invariably send the student back to your care. Here is the best truth I know about classroom discipline: If you throw a kid out of your class 30 times, they come back 31 ***(unless you win the teacher lottery, which is home schooling)!***

Remember these six lines of defense regarding classroom management:

The first line of defense is the student's ownership of, reflection on, suggested solutions to the issue, and demonstration of self-control. ***(Truly, there***

are some situations in which a kid will say. "I know what the problem is. Don't worry—I've got this!" And they take care of it. Give students a chance to BE the first line of defense.)

The second line is always the teacher.

Third is the parent or caregiver.

Fourth is the team.

Fifth is the counselor.

Sixth—and last—is the administrator. In most cases, teachers skip defense lines one through five and go directly to number six.

If teams use their own discipline process to take care of classroom management issues, student behaviors will change. If you want to build a positive classroom culture and good relationships with students, then handle everything that you can (and everything appropriate for you to handle) within the team. There is more consistency for the student. There are more (teachers') eyes on the student. Plus, all the other students on the team know and are required to meet the same expectations. This is a whole village pulling for each student to do well.

Teams need to set up a process to deal with student behaviors. But as they shape their discipline processes, they must be aware of the fine balance between what the team does and what administrators do. They must not overlook the need to discuss team plans with the administrator. **Teachers can't have the power to suspend kids anytime they feel like it. I was so angry once, I would have suspended a kid for eight weeks, when there were only four weeks of school left! And, let's be honest—that eight weeks of suspension doesn't really help anyway in most cases!**

Here are the kinds of discipline issues to anticipate and plan to handle as a team:

1. Tardies
2. Late work
3. No materials brought to class
4. Minor disruptions
5. Off-task behavior
6. No motivation

7. Cell phones
8. Ear buds
9. Minor arguments with other students
10. Running, pushing, and other normal adolescent behaviors
11. Minor language issues
12. Rudeness, disrespect
13. School dress code violations

Here are the kinds of discipline issues that are **not** for the team to handle:

1. Drugs
2. Weapons
3. Fighting
4. Potential danger to self or anyone else in the school
5. Behavior that typically leads to suspensions
6. Extreme language issues ***(We are hearing adolescents use more and more inappropriate language. We are shocked at how they use some very vulgar and sexually explicit language towards each other and the teachers.)***
7. Physical harm done to another student or a teacher ***(Please note: If a student picks up a chair and throws it at your head—that is definitely not a minor issue and should be handled by an administrator.)***
8. Vaping or other smoking
9. Inappropriate material, photos, or messages on their devices
10. Theft or destruction of property

When the circumstance **IS** something to pass on to an administrator, use a thoughtful process for making the referral. ***So many referrals are written in the heat of the moment, and in some cases, should never have been written. Team members should write a referral together, allowing them time to talk about the situation. There is a lot of power in a team referral. If a team writes a referral, perhaps bring the student into a team meeting (or to meet with one teacher) to discuss it before sending the referral and the student to the office.***

An idea to ponder: At the end of the school year, get together and review all the referrals written by the team members and sort them into three stacks:

Stack 1	Referrals that should have never been written
Stack 2	Referrals for issues that the team probably could have handled
Stack 3	Referrals that rightly were sent to the office

This is not meant to make our teammates feel bad. It is a reflection activity. It might help as you plan your discipline procedures for the next school year. Looking at those in Stack 2 can inspire you to be more courageous as a team to deal with some of the not-so-easy issues.

Construct Your Team Discipline Process

Great teams thoughtfully design a process for dealing with discipline incidents before they become big problems and for intervening when initial steps don't solve the issue. They take the time and energy to establish common protocols to deal with students and their progression of negative behaviors. Creating and implementing a comprehensive team discipline policy can avoid the common teacher complaint: "I sent them to the office and they did nothing!"

Here is a discipline process that I recommend:

Part 1: Minor Issues—Proactive Responses

Many minor issues can be addressed with a simple action, setting students on a positive track. Examples of these simple actions include

- A call to the parent or caregiver
- A meeting with a parent or caregiver, student, and teacher
- A teacher or team meeting with the student
- A talk between the student and a counselor or the student's advocate
- Some reflection time for the student
- The student identifying a strategy for solving the problem
- The student making amends with a conversation, an apology, a handshake to the other student or the teacher
- The student participating in some restorative practices

Keep track of the issue, the actions taken, the outcome, and follow up (along with dates). Enter notes in the student's file. (See Element 14 for details of record-keeping and documentation systems.)

Part 2: More Difficult, Persistent Issues—A Long-Term Intervention Plan

When the kinds of efforts above just don't work—even after your serious efforts—and the problem continues or worsens, it's time for a new tactic. Create a **TIPS Action Plan. (TIPS = Team Intervention Plan for the Student)**. This sets a specific four-week course of action with the goal of remedying the problem(s) and getting the student back on track.

Some parts of this plan will require advance preparation before the moment you need to put the process into action for a specific student. The team will need to gather workable ideas for intervention strategies, incentives or rewards, and follow-up procedures for the plan. To write out the details of a plan for a student, use Resource #18, "TIPS Planning Form," on page 207.

The TIPS Action Plan

Step 1 Get an overall view of the student.

Before making any plans for intervention, take time to get a broad view of what's going on with the student. Consider all the factors that affect the student, including social, emotional, academic, behavioral, and developmental issues, as well as outside influences. Use Resource #19 "Looking at All the Factors That Affect Students," on pages 208-209, as a guide. Asking the questions suggested on this resource can help your team focus closely on the whole picture of a student. Dialogue about this. Use the second page of this resource to make notes about the student in relation to each of the categories. This step serves as an informed, insightful base from which to understand the issues the student faces and move on to decisions about what to do next.

Step 2 Identify the issues and concerns.

Form a master list of the overall issues and concerns you see facing the student. Now, place these into two categories—academic and behavioral.

Step 3 Focus on specific concerns.

Choose **three** of those issues from **one** of the categories. Yes, the student may have 23 issues! But this plan will focus on three. Choose those that are most urgent or most "global" (affect several different areas of the student's success or well-being). Write these on your TIPS Planning Form (Resource #18). I advise that you do not intermix academic and behavioral issues. Though we as educators know that each influences the other, a young adolescent does not see the connections. So keep your TIPS Action Plan straightforward and easy for all to follow.

Step 4 Identify possible interventions or strategies.

Think about what will address the three particular issues and concerns you have selected for the student's plan. This is where your pre-discussed, pre-assembled list of interventions will serve you well! Choose **three to five** of those strategies. Some of the ideas might be for the teacher to implement and some are for the student's action. Think about the kinds of support the student may need; this may be specific materials, access to resources, or people outside the team to lend assistance. Have these ideas ready before putting the plan into action. See some suggestions on Resource #20, "Ideas for TIPS Action Plans," on page 210.

Step 5 Add follow-up ideas.

Generate ideas about how the team will follow up on the strategies. Choose **two or three.** These will be part of the plan. Also, decide how you will document the progress that you discover as you follow up. See some suggestions on Resource #20, "Ideas for TIPS Action Plans," on page 210.

Step 6 Choose incentives and rewards.

Think ahead about what may inspire the student to follow their prescribed tasks of the plan and how you will honor the student's improvement. What will keep the student working toward the goals? What will be given to the student as a symbol of their accomplishment?

Design tangible and immediate rewards and incentives for students (rewards for their completion or improvement on an issue—which also act as incentives to keep up the progress). These must be realistic. In so many cases, the rewards can be some extra time with the teacher or other students, or a lunch with teachers on the team to which the student can bring along a couple of friends. Or something as simple as this: Kids are thrilled to have a "high five" from all adult team members (or even other kids) for working hard to address an issue. ***We know that the satisfaction of completing the tasks or challenge or the visible improvement is the most important intrinsic reward for the student. But it's often also a joy for any kid to have a special moment or tangible reminder of the work.***

See some suggestions on Resource #20, "Ideas for TIPS Action Plans," on page 210. See samples of completed TIPS Plans on pages 115-116.

Step 7 Share the plan with students.

Discuss the plan with the student. Be sure the student has a thorough understanding of the plan and their responsibilities within it. In some cases, it might boost chances for the plan's success if the student contributes to the strategies or rewards and incentives.

Step 8 Go! Follow the plan.

Remember that this plan is to be implemented by the team **for at least four weeks.** Typically, we teachers cave far faster than our students. For real progress to be made, it is imperative to faithfully follow this plan for a dedicated period of time. The team can decide to extend the time if they feel it is worth doing so.

Step 9 Follow up and reward.

Do the follow-up! Great teams know that you must schedule several follow-up sessions with students. One of the most effective ways to change behavior is to bring a student into a team meeting after a week of implementing the plan. Let the student talk about what is working and what needs

TIPS Planning Form

(Team Intervention Plan for Students)

For Josie B Team Explorers Date 11/3

3 Issues Three behavioral issues

1 Use of cell phone in class

2 Refused to put cell phone away

3 Wearing ear buds in class

5 Strategies for moving forward

1 Josie will place her phone either in her backpack or in the clear pouch pocket at the front of the room.

2 Josie will be asked no more than three times to place the phone in one of those places; on the fourth time a call will be made to her home.

3 Josie can also choose to give the phone to the teacher if she prefers that option.

4 Josie will also place her ear buds in her backpack or in the clear pouch pocket at the front of the room.

5 Josie can choose to give her ear buds to the teacher during class time.

3 Ways to Follow Up

1 Josie will meet with the team once a week for four weeks to check the progress.

2 Mr. Berckemeyer will check in often to make sure she is following the plan.

3 When she does not comply, a phone call will be made to her home.

2 Incentives and Rewards

1 She can choose a reward each week from the team's reward system.

2 If she places her phone or ear buds in the correct place without reminders, she will get extra team tickets.

Student Signature ______________________

Parent or Caregiver Signature ______________________

Teacher Signature ______________________

TIPS Planning Form

(Team Intervention Plan for Students)

For Devon G. Team Dolphins Date 10/22

3 Issues Three academic Issues

1 Not completing work in Language Arts class

2 Missing assignments

3 No homework agenda

5 Strategies for moving forward

1 Devon will fill out the student agenda at the end of each class and show it to the teacher.

2 Devon will remain in Language Arts class until the work is completed.

3 A parent or caregiver will need to sign Devon's agenda every Monday.

4 Devon will stay after class or during lunch break with Mr. Berckemeyer on Monday and Wednesday to finish work.

5 For the next week, Devon will receive some modified LA assignments to help catch up with the unfinished and missing work.

3 Ways to Follow Up

1 Have Devon's advocate meet with him once a week.

2 Make a phone call giving Devon's family an update.

3 LA teacher will note how Devon did with the modifications.

2 Incentives and Rewards

1 Extra time to do assignments

2 Extra PBIS tickets

Student Signature ____________________

Parent or Caregiver Signature ____________________

Teacher Signature ____________________

adjustment. Include both one-on-one conversations and team follow-up sessions. Change happens when teachers provide ways for ongoing follow-up and coaching for students when they exhibit problem behaviors. This can include a structure to monitor ongoing progress, along with some rewards. Follow through on the planned rewards.

Step 10 Document the process.

Keep all forms and notes generated during the process. This will include the form you completed from Step 1, "Looking at All the Factors that Affect Students," a copy of the TIPS Planning Form, and a summary of what the teachers did, what the student did, and how the measures worked. It should also include dates and content of any meetings with the teacher or team, calls to parents and caregivers, or consultations with counselors who were part of the plan. Thorough documentation will build a complete picture of the issues, the intervention, and the outcomes. This will be critical to further steps that may need to be taken if behavior or issues become more severe. All this documentation goes into the student folder or Google doc. (See Element 14 for a more extensive discussion of documentation.)

During this entire process, make sure your administrator, essentials teachers, or counselors are providing support to the team as they create the plan and its strategies. There is nothing more frustrating than sending a student to the office only to have the administrators suggest five new ideas for dealing with the students. Lack of communication creates aggravation and frustration for the both the team and the administrators. Great administrators spend time in team meetings helping the team create ideas, so if the team referral is necessary, the administrators know the team has done everything in their power to change the student behavior.

Part 3: Particularly Persistent Issues (The "That-Did-Not-Work, Now What?" Plan)

Let's face it—there are times when our most dedicated use of proactive interventions just do not work. The academic, social, or behavioral issue may have intensified in frequency or severity, or the student and team may just be stuck. The student needs something more structured and extensive. A great team will try the TIPS plan for four to six weeks, document the progress, and then decide if it worked or if a next step needs to be created. This is different from the TIPS Action Plan in that it involves bringing more people into the process.

The "Now-What?" Plan could be a meeting with the student, team, parents or caregivers, administrator, and counselor. It may need to include a special ed teacher (if the student has one) or a psychologist. By the end of the meeting, the group will have agreed on a contract for the student's behavior—which will include clear, direct consequences for contract violations. The team can create consequences; these need to be enforced each time there is a violation to the contract.

Part 4: Administrative Decision

If the TIPS Action Plan, tried for several weeks, and the "Now What?" idea have failed, the case becomes an issue for the administrative team. The administrators will then create a plan for the student. Note: Your team should not be outsiders in this step. You will provide the administrators with clear documentation of all the measures the team has taken and the history of the situation. In addition, your team of teachers should be consulted in the creation of the administrators' plan and kept in the loop as to next steps for your student. This is still **your** student. And when parents and caregivers are involved in these scary, high-stakes decisions, they will feel more secure if a member of their child's team is part of the meetings.

Address Some Issues in Meetings with the Student

You'll notice that I mentioned using a team meeting with the student as a strategy to use in the process of dealing with minor issues, as well as more difficult discipline issues. Plan ahead for such meetings. ***Note: I have seen some really bad team meetings with students where teachers announce the 54 reasons that they are annoyed by the kid or the behaviors. Every teacher talks, repeating what others have said. The kid is beaten down so badly that the adult talk is tuned out.)***

By plan ahead, I mean consider these questions as a team before you bring a student into the meeting:

What is the purpose of the talk with the student?
What is the desired outcome?
Who will do the talking? (Never let everyone talk; it is unfair to the student. Never let everyone take a turn at saying something negative to the student.)
Will there be follow-up, a phone call home, a meeting with the parent or caregiver, an email to the counselor; or will the student come back in a week for follow-up?
How will you wrap up the meeting?

Then, when you hold the meeting:

- Select one person on the team to talk. This is best for the student, though it is hard for classroom teachers to do; we all feel the need to talk. **My friend, Judith Baenen, always reminds me that teachers constantly look for solutions and never really listen to the issues.** In many cases, the best person to do the talking (other than the student) is the advocate.
- Outline the discussion items with the student. Keep them simple and offer suggestions on how to change behaviors. If you have created or are creating a TIPS plan with the student, be sure the student has a copy of this and contributes to it.
- If the meeting is about academic matters, use your powers of technology to display the students' grades on your digital whiteboard. If the student has had referrals, project them as well. This helps keep the team and student focused on the data (evidence of the problem).
- When an issue is brought up and clarified in the meeting, begin by asking the student, **"Do you want us to Listen? To React? or To Solve??"** This is a good practice in lots of situations, including personal relationships—which is part of what is going on in a meeting with the student. This gives the person who is the focus of the meeting some control over what happens.
- Ask how the student or the teacher can fix some of the damage done. Discuss this with the student.

The meeting should take fewer than five minutes.

AVOID THESE ACTIONS

In this chapter, you've read about what to do to put Element 10 into action. Here's a quick list of some things **not** to do.

As you work to **design and use a consistent team discipline process**, steer clear of

1. Creating a policy that is hard for students or parents and caregivers to understand.
2. Working through a policy without discussing it with your teaming administrator.
3. Including vague or unrealistic expectations (or procedures for students to reach them).
4. Neglecting to plan a clear intervention for more severe or repeated discipline issues.
5. Forgetting about the six lines of defense—particularly the first two.
6. Writing an individual TIPS Action Plan without involving the student.
7. Failing to share the complete policy with students and their families—in writing—along with the rationale behind the expectations.
8. Conducting team meetings with a student without listening to the student's take on the issue and asking for their ideas for resolution.
9. Forgetting to review and re-evaluate your discipline procedure policy at least twice yearly.

ELEMENT 11

Keep a Razor Focus on Kids

The Successful Middle School: This We Believe
Characteristics Crossover

- Every student's academic and personal development is guided by an adult advocate.
- Policies and practices are student-centered, unbiased, and fairly implemented.
- Organizational structures foster purposeful learning and meaningful relationships.

Great teams constantly keep students at the center of the spotlight. Their goals, actions, and care are all about doing what helps students thrive.

WHY THIS ELEMENT IS ESSENTIAL

The entire school community enjoys plenty of benefits when teams consistently attend to what will help **the kids** best learn, develop, and succeed in school.

Here's what I see in schools where this element is done well:

- Teachers know what it means to focus on kids. They get the difference between talking and venting about kids and planning strategies to help kids. Student issues and needs really do get addressed in team meetings. Teams find solutions and put them to work.
- Teams examine their biases together. They commit to treating students equitably, without displaying (openly or subtly) different attitudes or expectations to different students.
- Students like that the adults want to know them (even if they may not openly

admit it). They are comfortable around their teachers and feel that their teachers on the team like them.

- Students clearly know who's there to talk to when they have an issue; they head straight for the personal advocate. They are confident that they can get help, and so they are more likely to seek it.
- Students don't fall through the cracks. There are fewer late homework papers, forgotten assignments, and situations where a kid gets so far behind that they can't catch up. There are fewer cases of lost, confused, or disconnected students.
- Individual teachers are secure in knowing that they don't have to be the only advocate for all the students in their classes.
- Parents and caregivers know that their kids feel known and welcomed by every adult team member. The work on relationships spreads to the families. Parents and caregivers feel more trust in the school.

HOW TO PUT THIS ELEMENT INTO ACTION

Until we can make sure that middle grades teachers genuinely enjoy being around young adolescents, really make them the center of the whole enterprise, and provide adequate, personal advocacy for them, we are spinning our wheels instead of accomplishing many of our goals. This is why AMLE emphasizes the importance of student advocacy, boldly spreading the belief that having teachers who are committed to young adolescents is an essential part of the middle school model. (See *The Successful Middle School, This We Believe*[14].)

Of course, this is not just about middle school. "Focusing on kids"—really attending to their development and needs and nurturing relationships with them—should be a mantra for all schools. I hope this chapter is a call to action for schools, all teachers, all teams, at all levels, to focus our visions, our goals, and our teamwork squarely on the students. Maybe it is time for us to rise and say, "**Our** school! **Our** team! **Our** kids!"

Focus on the Kids

"But we thought we already were focused on kids!" Just about every school, team, or teacher insists that the students are the top priority. It's even written in most schools' mission statements and in the vision or philosophy for many teams. We think we are focused on kids. We mean to be. Did you know that most teams spend the majority of their meeting time talking about kids? They do—as much as 60% or more.

> **Yes, it is true that kids are our main focus, and that in many cases, they are easy to talk about—because they can be our common frustration. Therefore, it's painless to complain and enumerate their latest escapades and antics. The problem comes when teams consume their time repeatedly unleashing their annoyances about the same student (or handful or students). Nothing changes.**

There's the problem. Much of all that talking time about kids is spent venting. It's the tale-telling: "You'll never believe what Melissa did this week." It's commiserating about student behavior or family noncooperation. It's lamenting the lack of consistency, responsibility, or improvement. Even worse, all that time is not even about **all** the kids; 95% of the time teams **do** talk about kids, they talk about just 5% of the student population. Remember the norm that I mentioned in Element 7 for team meetings? I'll repeat my preaching about this important rule: You are allowed three free vents for a student. The fourth venting comment about this student must be ideas for a solution to whatever the issue is.

To deepen the problem, often not nearly enough of the talking is about solutions. Teams need to spend their time **doing** instead of talking—taking such actions as these:

- Identifying the specific issues or behaviors that need to be addressed.
- Outlining strategies to address specific issues.
- Planning a way to redirect behavior for that kid.
- Inviting a student to a team meeting to talk about concrete steps the student can take.
- Planning how to combine all adult efforts to tackle a problem.
- Giving a student a pep talk.
- Meeting with parents or caregivers to plan strategies for improvement.
- Writing up a team intervention action plan for the student.

- Re-meeting with the student to see how the plan worked.
- Making a team phone call home to provide information, ideas, and support to parents and caregivers.

If teams take such actions, they'll find that they can reduce the amount of time they spend talking in futility. They'll be using their time effectively and efficiently to find real answers and kick off real changes. ***Though we may think of ourselves as focused on our students, it's often the case that we rarely talk with teammates or colleagues about what that means. And even more rare are the times that we check up on ourselves to see if we really are focusing on students.***

Decide What It Really Means to Be "Focused on Kids"

Focusing on kids means intentionally and continually tuning into their needs, changes, behaviors, progress, and challenges. It means seeing them as individuals and as a group. And it means acting on what you see.

Here are 20 signs that a team has **kids** at the center of its vision, heart, and goals:

1. All team members get to know all the students.
2. Team members are very knowledgeable about the intellectual, social, emotional, moral, ethical, and physical **characteristics and needs** of the developmental age of their students.
3. Each team member communicates to students without bias, ridicule, shame, sarcasm, or judgment.
4. The team spends time understanding and discussing the major issues challenging young adolescents and learning ways to help students find support to deal with these.
5. The team has a vision statement soundly built on their beliefs about students and are committed to actualizing it to meet student needs.
6. The team has a specific plan for how they will get to know each student well—academically, personally, socially, and emotionally.
7. Team members are committed to cultivating trusting relationships with

students and among students. The team identifies and practices specific strategies to do this.

8. Each team member greets each student on the team energetically and positively any time they meet.
9. You will often hear team members ask one another—in many situations—such questions as: "Is this good for the students?" "Will this further our goals for our students?" "Will this help the students become better learners?" "Will this increase academic success, social development, or independence for students?" Everything passes through the "Is it good for kids?" filter!
10. Team members speak respectfully to and about the students and their families.
11. Team members make concerted efforts to differentiate instruction so that students have opportunities to learn in ways best for them.
12. The team has clearly articulated academic expectations for students. Team members regularly help students reach these expectations.
13. Student efforts and successes are recognized regularly. Teams plan celebrations to recognize and encourage all kinds of team and individual student accomplishments.
14. Students feel emotionally and physically safe in their team environments.
15. Every student on the team is discussed at a team meeting at least twice during the year. The team takes a comprehensive overview of the student's progress and wellbeing.
16. The team consciously plans ways for students to have input into classroom policies, procedures, problem solving, and learning experiences. Students on a team will say they have a voice and many choices in classroom life and learning.
17. Team members act to help students fit in and polish social skills.
18. All students' families are an important part of the learning community. Team members cultivate positive, trusting relationships with families.
19. Every student has one adult advocate assigned specifically to them.

20. Teams work together to build a list of ways to advocate for students. They share their advocacy ideas and experiences.

Build Meaningful Relationships

You may be wondering why I waited until near the end of the book to talk about relationships. After all, without great relationships, nothing will ever work. If an administrator does not work well with the staff, no new programs will be developed. If teachers cannot get along and instead spend their time committing educational sabotage, then teacher spirit will decline. If teachers cannot build strong, trusting relationships with students, then both teachers and students will struggle to succeed.

Building relationships is not meant to be at the front or at the end of this book. It is meant to happen throughout the whole process of teaming. Everything that I have written in this book is ultimately about relationships.

Caring relationships are at the heart of a student-focused team. A large body of research shows that the bonds of positive teacher-student relationships give students a secure base for social and academic development over many years. Strong, healthy teacher-student relationships are associated with improvements on practically every measure important to schools: attendance, behavior, dropout rates, motivation, achievement levels, academic tenacity, and school belonging and satisfaction.[15]

But the need for quality relationships in the school and on teams is about more than the teacher-student relationships. Peer encounters play powerful roles in the lives of students. These contacts and connections are major factors in any student's experience and success. In the presence of safe, trusting relationships, peers can provide for each other a sense of belonging, emotional and social support, practice in prosocial behavior, opportunities for reducing bias, models for self-management, settings for cooperative learning, and support for taking on academic challenges.[16] With supportive peer relationships, students fare better in all aspects of school. And the impact of peer relationships increases as students proceed into middle school and high schools.[17]

One marvelous thing about teaming is this: A team of adults working together is a living model of quality relationships. It's an example of learning and growing together. Robust learning happens for us, too, in the presence of our significant relationships with students and other team members. And by the way, when kids witness satisfying and caring teacher-student relationships and healthy relationships among the adults on the team, they tend to copy these behaviors in their connections with their peers.

On the other hand, if we don't work hard to build good relationships with our students and teammates and to teach kids how to relate to one another, I guarantee we'll see these outcomes:

- Young adolescents will have to navigate school without the security of knowing caring adults are looking out for their best interests.
- Classroom management and behavior problems will be frequent.
- Kids' motivation and engagement in schoolwork will wane.
- Many students will exhibit stress, disengagement, and unruliness.
- Teacher morale will decline.
- Students' academic progress will fall short of their potential.

Earlier in this chapter, one of the items on the list of signs that the team has focused on kids (earlier in this chapter) was this:

> Team members are committed to cultivating trusting relationships with students and among students. **The team identifies and practices specific strategies to do this.**

Notice the second sentence. Meaningful, impactful relationships throughout the team must be more than an intention. The team must **act** on this priority—learning and intentionally using techniques, then reflecting on how well they're doing at this goal. This includes knowing the fads, fashions, trends, and slang. It means being aware of students' media anxiety, social groups, gender identification, and peer influences.

There are many ways to make sure we are connecting with our kids and helping them learn to have healthy connections with one another. There are even ways to encourage the most reluctant teachers to build relationships with the most reluctant students. This is a topic for your team meetings and for your team's professional development.

Advocate Fiercely

This may seem like an unusual goal: to actually start caring about students and showing it by being their advocates! After all, we are teachers. Aren't teachers all about kids? Well, that's what we like to think. **Advocacy is an active result of relationship-building,** and it is a key foundation of effective teaming and the middle school model. It's the way to show students that not one of them is ever alone or disconnected. It's the way to keep kids in school, on track, coping, and succeeding academically. If we don't see the action, we should probably question the statement, "We're all about the kids."

Advocacy requires connection. And when a teacher sees 120 students a day, it becomes a lofty goal to make connections with every student. Yes, we can all work at healthy relationships with students and each other. And we can all advocate to the best of our abilities for every student on the team in minor or major ways throughout a school day and year. We can teach kids to advocate for themselves and each other. But each one of us on the team cannot possibly build a close relationship with, keep tabs on, run interference for, shore up, or help solve problems with every student on the team at all times.

That's why I want to wrap up this element with a great technique to build deep relationships and set in motion a system where every student has at least one adult advocate who guides their academic and personal development.

The Index Card Activity

This activity matches each student with an advocate on your team. Then it allows teachers to connect with those students for whom they will advocate, and commits to a policy that every child will have regular communications with an adult. (It is not about an advisory group, house, or a homeroom. In many cases, students are in those classes because a computer selected them. This is a system where real live teachers choose to connect with specific students.) The following activity shows ways to make those connections (see Step Nine below).

The Index Card Activity is done about four to six weeks into the school year. It is most effective when all team members take part in this activity. However, it can be done by an individual teacher. (I will explain how an individual teacher can use the advocacy concept using just their own class roster.) See Resource #21, "The Index Card Activity," on page 211.

Step 1

Write every student's first and last name on an index card. Use large letters so everyone can see the name on the card. If you have 120 kids on your team, then you should have 120 index cards. Instead of writing the cards, you can print labels from the school database and stick them on the cards. Or, even better, have students create their own. Make this a getting-to-know-you activity. Ask students to write their names on a card in large, readable letters. Then, tell them to use the back of the card to add three things about themselves that they'd like the teachers to know.

Step 2

Place all the cards on the table, face up, with every name visible.

Step 3

As a gesture of respect for our veteran teachers, have the most experienced teacher on the team choose one student by picking up the index card. Teachers should pick a student who they have come to know; a student who makes them smile; a student with whom they'd like to connect; or a student who might give them anxiety—but in a fun way! ***To be blunt, this is mostly about picking kids you like.***

Step 4

Once you pick the card, you must explain to the team why you picked that student. Just give a couple of examples. ***Let's not make this a three-minute diatribe on the attributes of the students—just a few quick words.***

Step 5

Have the next most experienced teacher pick a student and explain why. Continue with other team members choosing student cards. Repeat this four times for each team member.

Step 6

Complete several speed rounds with each teacher picking three names per turn. Continue for three or four rounds. Team members do not need to explain why they picked each student, unless they want to. Your goal is to get down to about 20 cards left on the table.

Step 7

Once there are about 20 names left on the table, stop and have everyone on the team look at the names they have chosen. Each teacher asks, "Are there patterns in the characteristics of the students I've picked?" For example, one teacher noted, "I am picking all the athletes." Well, that made sense; she was the volleyball and softball coach.

Then, look at the names that are left on the table. Ask, "Why has each of these students not been selected? Is it because no one on the team knows the student? Or is it because no one on the team likes the student? Or is it because the student is a behavior problem?" Looking at the collective group of cards not taken may give the team some clues that they have a bias towards some types of students.

Recently, I had a team take part in this activity. At this point in the process, they noticed that all their special education students were left (not picked). They realized that as a team, they had a bias against these students. They proceeded to figure out why and then took steps to correct that situation.

Step 8

Now look at the cards left on the table, one by one. Ask yourselves, "What does this student need?" For example, some students need a Loving Mama person; others might need a Loving Mama with a little sternness; another student may need a positive, male role model. **(well heck, I even fit two out of three of those categories. I'm just not sure which two)**. Several of the kids might need a village, small city, or large city to be their advocate. All the team members might take a copy of that card! Continue until every one of the students is chosen by a teacher.

Step 9

Once you have your set of cards, choose five to seven of those cards every week. Be sure you make natural connections with those students. Check up on them, ask them how they're doing, talk about the weather or sports. Keep your eye on these kids through other teachers and any online reports on work or behavioral issues that may arise. Get an overview of the general status for each kid—of their homework and assignment completion, grades, work habits. Know about accomplishments, absences, habitual tardies, their highs and lows, or any family, academic, behavioral, or social assets and difficulties. Step in to help students get extra guidance or assistance they may need from school staff outside the team.

Rotate the cards through the weeks, so that you make contact with and get a general overview of all the students on your list over a period of a few weeks. If you are a teacher doing this Index Card Activity on your own, take the top five names on the roster from each class. Make a connection with these students at some point during the week. The next week, do the same with the next five names.

Here are some hints for making this strategy work:

- All team members must remember that just because each teacher is the assigned advocate for a set of specific students, this does not mean that the rest of you stop showing interest in other students. We all want to build the best relationships we can with each one; each student should see evidence that each teacher thinks they are welcome, valued, and worth getting to know. It's wonderful for all students to realize they have a whole team surrounding and supporting them.

- After several weeks, you may need to trade a student to another teacher advocate. A natural connection might not have developed between the two of you, but could with another teacher.
- When picking the last 20 kids, teachers may not end up with the same number of students. A little variation in the quantities doesn't matter; it is about quality of the connections.
- As a team, reflect again on the 20 students who were not picked in the first several rounds. Take a little more time to talk about why. If you do this together, you may be able to offer ideas or insights to the teachers who now have those kids on their list.

  During work at a school in Pennsylvania, I had a teacher on one of the teams who was a little reluctant to do the Index Card Activity. I asked him to please participate as a favor to me and the team, and he did. When the 20 cards were left, he got quiet and seemed upset. When I asked him why, he responded, "What if my child were one of those students left on the table?" This was an eye-opening experience for everyone. It made the whole process real. These are real kids who need someone to care for them and watch out for them.
- After a while, you can also use those index cards to form team groups for field trips, or you can make them your homeroom group.
- Once a week at a team meeting, teams will ask each teammate to talk about **three** of their index-card kids, sometimes asking they only share nonacademic items about the child.
- **Here's an important reminder: Students do not and should not know about the Index Card Activity.** Teachers absolutely cannot walk into a classroom after the team has completed the activity and say something like, "We picked kids we liked today," or even, "At our team meeting yesterday, each teacher picked the kids to be on their advocate lists." It will quickly become awkward when a student says, "Did you pick me?" ***So, this also means not putting on the top of a large poster: "Kids I really like," laminating it, and displaying it next to your classroom door.***

This index card strategy may seem simple, but it creates a powerful touchstone that will make a striking difference for your team and students. And it is a tangible tool for every adult team member to compel us to keep ongoing, meaningful connections with our students.

AVOID THESE ACTIONS

In this chapter, you've read about what to do to put Element 11 into action. Here's a quick list of some things **not** to do.

As you **plan ways to keep and show your focus on kids,** steer clear of

1. Failing as a team to seriously evaluate the amount of time you spend **talking about kids** instead of **making proactive plans** for them.
2. Overlooking the powerful influence that teacher's relationships (with students and with other teachers) have on students' relationships with one another.
3. Underestimating the absolute necessity and incredible benefits of assigning one adult advocate to each student.
4. Avoiding being the advocate for a kid you don't know or think might take too much effort to oversee.
5. Hurrying through or hopping over Step 7 in the Index Card Activity (discussing the last 20 name cards left on the table).
6. Ignoring my bold-type reminder about not letting students know about the Index Card Activity.

ELEMENT 12

Make Academic Success Checks a Habit

The Successful Middle School: This We Believe
Characteristics Crossover

- Every student's academic and personal development is guided by an adult advocate.
- Organizational structures foster purposeful learning and meaningful relationships.

Great teams take intentional steps to keep students from stalling or sliding behind in their academic progress. They regularly check for specific lapses, issues, or stumbling blocks to student success, and they plan interventions to rectify the issues as quickly as possible.

WHY THIS ELEMENT IS ESSENTIAL

All members of the school community reap numerous benefits when the teams consistently monitor the state of students' academic work and take swift actions to address problems or needs.

Here's what I see in schools where this element is done well:

- When students stumble with their work, they get help right away. Small problems with their lack of progress don't turn into big problems.
- Together, teachers from all disciplines have rewarding opportunities to work together toward the academic success of every student on the team.
- Students are more comfortable coming to class, because they are not hopelessly behind in their understanding or assignments.

- No student goes unseen during the quarterly academic checks.
- Teachers love the ease and effectiveness of the Thumbs-Up, Thumbs-Down sessions.
- Parents and caregivers are relieved to see that the team is on top of their child's schoolwork status.
- Leaders see fewer kids sink into downward spirals of incompletes and failures.

HOW TO PUT THIS ELEMENT INTO ACTION

Student academic achievement is a top goal for any school or team. One of the reasons we structure schools around teams is to do the best possible job of boosting academic success for students. All the essential elements of teaming in this book, when done effectively, contribute to this aim. When students learn in a team format, not one, but a group of teachers, combine their care, insights, and ideas to make sure the kids on their team get and stay on a path to academic success. This chapter is about a super strategy that I've seen work for many teams—a strategy to notice and act on signals that a student might be falling off that path.

Start Regular Academic Success Checks

In my work with hundreds of schools and teams, I have found these things to be true when it comes to keeping students on track with their work:

1. Teams mainly discuss the students whose needs or behavior stand out most. That robs teachers of the team-time to examine how all the kids on the team are doing academically.
2. In some cases, a teacher never knows if a student on the team is missing assignments or giving other signals of academic slide in classes other than their own. There's no planned effort to check to see if the same problems are showing up in another class.
3. Teams have as many as 120 ***(or more, yikes!)*** students. Teachers can't imagine how they can possibly talk about the academic status of all those kids during team meetings. So, the team overviews don't happen.

The "Academic Success Checks" process is a strategy that solves all three of these problems for a team. This process is also known as the "Thumbs-Up, Thumbs-Down" strategy or the "Weeks 3, 5, and 7 Plan." The general idea of the process is this:

Team members identify a topic (indicator) related to learning and working habits and agree to discuss how every student on the team is doing with that indicator. This can be any practice that you know contributes to success for the student. Or it can be a signal or symptom of lapses or difficulties. These might be such things as poor organization of academic work, missing work, chronically late assignments, missed assignments, work that is turned in but only minimally completed, or work that shows the student is not understanding the material. Sixth-graders new to middle school might need the first-quarter topic to be finding their way around the building and opening their lockers. The topics and the length of focus on a topic will be fluid, depending on student need. Teachers on the team will know what topics to choose.

For my description of this strategy, I'll use this topic: missing assignments. At least twice each quarter (three times if possible), the team will check to make sure students are not missing a large number of assignments (across all subjects). I'm using this example because I've noticed that, if a student is missing three or more assignments across multiple subjects by Week 3 of the quarter, by Weeks 5 and 7 they'll have more than a 70% chance of failing the quarter.

In some cases, students might have more than 100 assignments due in nine weeks. And if they start off missing three or more assignments within the first several weeks, they still have another 70 assignments to go before the end of the quarter. As we teachers know, when kids get seriously behind with work, they get overwhelmed, and it seems impossible to catch up. Teams must attack the trend of missing work quickly and effectively for the student to pass the quarter. ***If not, it will be about Week 7, Day 2 of the quarter that the parent or caregiver calls, asking for all the missing work. You'll oblige the request but will be bitter at the copy machine for duplicating all this missing work that you're pretty sure is never coming back.***

So, at three points during each quarter (for example, at Weeks 3, 5, and 7), great teams will do an Academic Success Check on all their students. Do your best to get your first checkup in at Week 3. This really helps decrease overall failure rates and sets a consistent pattern for academic oversight. For a quick guide to the academic success check process, see Resource #22, "Thumbs Up, Thumbs Down," on page 212.

The Strategy at Work

Step 1

Every two or three weeks team meeting times should be dedicated to determining if any students are missing three or more assignments in multiple subjects. ***(Preferably they meet in weeks 3, 5, and 7—allowing students time to finish up work missing at week 7 before the end of the quarter.)*** Knowing that this will be the topic for check-up, teachers should come to the checkup meeting with strategies for how to remedy this problem. Note that teachers may choose to widen the topic of missing assignments to also include work that is chronically late, is done haphazardly, or shows signs that the student is floundering with the material.

Step 2

Gather an alphabetic list of the team's students. ***(That's right—all the students. If you have 120 on the team, there will be that many names!)*** Remind teachers to bring records of grades or any other information about students' academic status. Do not cheat the process and only bring the names of students with all D's and F's.

Step 3

With the entire team of teachers gathered, say each name in order out loud. Give the student a **thumbs-up** if they are doing okay—that is, **not** missing three or more assignments in your subject. If a student is missing three or more assignments in your class, you give them a **thumbs-down.** Feel free to ask the essentials teachers to send a list of students with three or more missing assignments in their classes. This is a good way to support those classes outside the team as well as within.

Step 4

If only one teacher has given thumbs-down, then it's up to that teacher to choose an action for dealing with the issue of missing assignments. However, if the student has multiple thumbs-down responses, their name goes on a list of students who need some intervention.

Step 5

Once the team has made the list of students who need attention for this issue, the team chooses strategies to help students catch up on their work. This will take some personalization. One size does not fit all when choosing student strategies because students will be behind for different reasons. The team will have to select the right strategy for each student. That doesn't mean 25 different strategies, necessarily. There may be one or two that work for most. Also, before the team leaves this meeting, they'll need to be clear about who is responsible to see that each of the strategies is put into place and who will monitor the progress.

Notes:

- This process must move quickly, with no side conversations. If, after naming each student, you talk about that student, the task will take 6 weeks instead of 20 minutes. ***For example, if the team says the name Bernice Buttstrom and everyone has a comment about the kid, you all can kiss the idea of an efficient process goodbye.***
- Remember, for students to be placed on the intervention list (for this example), they must have three or more missing assignments in multiple subjects.

Sample Interventions

Once the team has formed the list of names, it takes time, ideas, and planning to help each student get caught up and off the list. The team needs to create a list of ideas and strategies to use with the students who are missing three or more assignments in multiple subjects. That will provide a selection of ideas that can be fitted to different students. Below are some suggestions to get you started. Be sure to keep a record of the intervention used for each student. Enter this into your communication log. (See Element 15 for details.) You might design a template to keep a master list of the names, interventions, and follow-up for your team records. See an example of this, Resource #23, "Academic Success Check, Team Record," on page 213.

Try these strategies:

- Make a phone call to the student's home. Note: This is one that may not work for all students. Some parents and caregivers are supportive and willing to help. Some might be angry that you called and not be helpful; the call might make things worse for the student. As you get to know your students well, your teachers will learn for which students this will work and for which it won't. There's no need to add more trauma to a student's life.
- Have kids come into one of the team classrooms for an after-school session or during lunch break. Teachers can rotate overseeing these.
- A couple of times a week, schedule a session over lunch during which students from a higher grade level of high school can not only supervise, but help and encourage.
- During class time, after school, or on lunch break, let kids with same or similar assignments work in pairs or small groups on their own. They can challenge each other to get the work done quickly and right. An adult would be present, but kids would have the responsibility for seeing that the whole group does it well.
- Have the student's advocate work with the student. For example, a student might not be missing any work in the advocate's class, so the advocate can get a list of what's missing and encourage the student to do the work in their class, under their supervision. We all know that some kids will work well for certain teachers and not for others. Let's be real: If a student is missing eight total assignments from various classes, do we really care how or where the work gets done or who supervises?

- If there are many students on the list, maybe the team can have a catch-up and enrichment day during the team time. Have several teachers work with students who are missing work and have one do some enrichment activities with the students who are caught up. Let me be clear: Enrichment is not eating pizza and watching *Finding Nemo* (a movie they've all seen at least five times because it's one of the few that appeases all families). ***They've all eaten pizza and found Nemo.*** Do something instructive—blow stuff up, investigate something outside, have game time, or do a compassion project where the students make cards for the local nursing home or write notes to police officers to thank them for doing a tough job. Please note: These sessions should not affect the essential classes. Work the schedule so that students still get to those classes.
- Here's a strategy that might surprise you; hopefully, it will intrigue. I've seen it work very well: Let's keep a student in the room until their work is done. Of course, apply the one-size-does-not-fit-all rule to this. Never hold the student who might be a massive disruption. Choose students who can do the work without a lot of teacher help—those who know the material and can do it, but have just have let it slide.

  This idea will likely warrant some time to discuss as a team, grade level, and building. But first let me ask a simple question: Are you, like most educators, appalled that we socially promote children who continuously fail? If your answer is yes, then let me ask you this: What do we do when a student who **can** do the work refuses to work and then the bell rings? We let them go the next class. So, in many ways we socially promote students every day, every hour, every class period. We let them leave at the end of class without having done the work. ***In essence, we broadcast this message: "If you don't work, then we reward you by letting you leave and go on to the next class." We might as well hang a banner in the school halls that says, "Achievement is based on a bell."***
- There may be times when a student's backlog is so overwhelming that you'll need to take an approach that does not entail the student doing the whole of every assignment. Since the point of the work is to understand a concept or master a skill or process—you could ask some questions (or have the kid

solve a few problems) from the failed or missing assignment to determine if the material is understood. (Do this in person with the student.) Correct answers would allow for a passing, rather than a failing, grade in the whole class. For example, a student may have low scores, say 15% on a few of the assignments. Mathematically this could make it almost impossible to increase the overall percentages for the quarter. But the grade could move up to, say, a 59%, based on answering key questions or completing key parts. It changes the "super F" into something closer to passing.

This is not a case of raising the grade for doing nothing. This is asking the student to do some of an assignment better than it was done, and thus giving the student a fighting chance for the quarter. It's a way to knock off some of that huge stack of unsatisfactory or missing work.

- Take advantage of any interventions or other support systems your school may already have in place for students with the particular issue you have identified for your Academic Success Checks.
- Document students' responses to the intervention strategies. If one isn't working well for a student or group of students, try a new one.

AVOID THESE ACTIONS

In this chapter, you've read about what to do to put Element 12 into action. Here's a quick list of some things **not** to do.

As you**, plan and carry out Student Academic Success Checks,** steer clear of

1. Using strategies or explanations that might make the students on the catch-up list feel embarrassed, dumb, or shamed.
2. Letting more than three weeks lapse between academic success checkups.
3. Letting a student have four failing grades in the quarter.
4. Discussing individual kids during the Thumbs Up-Thumbs Down process.
5. Doing the Academic Success Checks without having a good supply of intervention strategies ready.
6. Giving too little attention to monitoring the strategies.

ELEMENT 13

Cooperate on Curriculum

The Successful Middle School: This We Believe
Characteristic Cross-Over

- Curriculum is challenging, exploratory, integrative, and diverse.
- Instruction fosters learning that is active, purposeful, and democratic.
- Organizational structures foster purposeful learning and meaningful relationships.

Great teams break down boundaries among subject areas taught by team members and collaborate to find ways to interconnect the content, processes, and skills.

WHY THIS ELEMENT IS ESSENTIAL

The entire school community enjoys a variety of positive learning outcomes when teams give serious attention to correlating many aspects of the content areas taught by the team.

Here's what I see in schools where this element is done well:

- Teachers don't have to re-teach as often.
- Students are free from having many different methods for the same learning processes.
- Teachers show deep understanding and appreciation for the professional skills of their teammates.
- Teachers on the teams are better at their craft. They share and polish

teaching strategies and learn from each other. They work together to help students meet high expectations and succeed academically.

- Students get the benefit of good instructional practices that teachers have found effective and shared with each other.
- Students are proud to accomplish the team's 10-Day Learning Goals.
- Parents and caregivers see that their child is making connections in their learning.
- School leaders see teachers stretching beyond their specific subject areas to make cross-discipline connections.

HOW TO PUT THIS ELEMENT INTO ACTION

Some of the most powerful effects of teaming result from the curriculum connections made among the subject areas covered by the team.[18] That's the point of interdisciplinary teams! Students learn skills, processes, and concepts that cross content areas and can be used with these subjects and many others. They see how the same big ideas show up in many different topics. And, they are involved in learning activities that have a variety of strong, correlated instructional approaches.

Cross-discipline learning is a major part of the teaming concept. One of the biggest concerns I have right now in education is about how we have bunkered curriculum in middle schools. But the more time we spend talking to each other within our subject-areas, the less likely we are to make the curriculum connections among subject areas that our students desperately need. Our students may be learning the content, but they struggle to apply the content outside of that class.

Even within a school teaming model, teams are too often teams in name only. The potential power of what students can gain with true interdisciplinary coordination is lost. Many big concepts and learning practices remain fragmented—even confusing or conflicting. Just as kids benefit when we get rid of scattered expectations for classroom life, so they flourish when we plan consistencies and linkages for what they learn and how they learn it. What one teacher on the team teaches is used, applied, and reinforced in all the other classes. It's a beautiful process to behold!

Change How Team Time Is Spent

Too often, the topics that consume most of team-meeting discussion time *(pains me to say this)* are **not** related to planning how to set and help students reach high expectations, or how to provide the kind of coordinated learning experiences that raise achievement. As I have mentioned before, a large chunk of team time is spent talking about kids—and most of that time, about only a few kids. (And most of **that** time, few solutions or actual plans of action are reached.) The outcomes: 1. Achievement does not improve. 2. Teacher morale declines.

It is not necessary to plan intricate interdisciplinary units of study to reap the benefits of curriculum connection I've just described. It just takes a commitment on the part of the teachers to use team time to coordinate concepts and instructional practices. This is why great teams spend at least 25% of their team time on curriculum. They dedicate this time to curriculum correlations and adamantly protect it. To do this effectively, teams must carefully plan those agendas and stick with them. They must resist the temptation to spend too much time on housekeeping chores and venting.

All team members need to know what every other team member is planning: the topics, themes, standards, and concepts; kinds of activities; teaching strategies; student expectations; homework; assessments; materials; and special events. And team members need to know how all this fits into the calendar. A focus on curriculum, instruction, and calendar connections meets all these needs.

A good place for your team to start with this element is to take time before school begins (or as early in the year as possible) to brainstorm about the kinds of curriculum, instructional, and calendar connections that might work for your subject areas and grade levels. Start a list. You'll want to add to this and adapt components as the year goes along, but it's good to have an ample reserve of good ideas at the beginning. That way you'll be ready to follow the connection strategies below during your team time. For inspiration to get going on your own lists, see Resource, #24, "Ways to Connect Curriculum," on page 214.

Make Curriculum Connections

1. Come to the meeting ready to share descriptions of these with your teammates:
   Topics, themes, big ideas to be taught
   Specific skills to focus on (i.e., writing essays, research skills, taking notes)
   Key vocabulary related to content
   Homework load and schedule
   Project expectations for students
   Tests and quizzes
   Teaching strategies and types of learning activities planned
   Standards to cover
   Special events (such as field trips or presentations)
   - When giving an overview of your curriculum and instruction plans, provide other team members with any vocabulary or spelling lists students will get for the week. ***You might even share a graphic organizer that you plan to use in your class, hoping that your teammates might use it as well for the week. This helps with consistency for students, and, let's be honest—do students really need to use seven different graphic organizers on the same skill in a week?***
   - Provide all team members a copy of any tests or quizzes you plan to give, along with the study guides you have given students.
   - Share any reading assignments, stories, challenging math problems, or research or investigation steps your students will be expected to complete.
2. Keep a team calendar for the week, showing what is being taught and expected of students (the elements listed in #1 above). Post this on the team website. If students in your school use a standard student planner, project a page from that planner that you have filled in with the assignments, requirements, and events from the week's team calendar. (Students can transfer the information into their personal planners. Make sure it has each teacher's homework listed on the correct date.)
3. Step back and pause to look at the curricular areas and concepts from each teacher.
   - Look for places where curriculum can be aligned—where one concept or skill can be strengthened across all disciplines. Talk about how you can enhance this connection. Look for ways to parallel teach a concept.

- Do a quick brainstorm of ways to connect curriculum in the upcoming week. Look for big concepts and general skills that apply to all content areas.
- Look for ways to modify an assignment or project to connect it to something another teacher is teaching. Ask each other for examples and ideas.
- Look for possible vocabulary connections. Are there terms that relate to multiple subject areas in upcoming plans?

Make Instructional Connections

1. Talk about the kinds of activities you intend to use for students. Describe the kinds of instructional strategies you have planned.
2. Step back and look at the calendar again.
    - Rearrange or change instructional plans to complement the kinds of experiences students will have in other subject areas. **(For example, if you see that all four or five of you planned to build a clay model of something—a few of you might want to switch your plans!)**
    - Try to arrange the days so that students have a healthy variety of learning adventures.
    - Discuss practices that have been successful. Try new strategies. Keep every discussion or selection of instructional practices focused on improving chances for students to achieve.
    - Once a month, have a team member share a teaching strategy that has worked well to engage students. This can be as simple as a writing prompt, rubric of criteria for a skill, graphic organizer, great meme, short video, or a creative way to group kids for an activity.
    - Talk about the standards you plan to cover. Try to touch on the same standard across all disciplines. Discuss ways you can deepen that standard with joint efforts.
3. Look for specific skills that pertain to some of the topics and tasks across the week's curriculum. Be sure to teach, review, and use those in each class. Some might work into your 10-Day Learning Goals. (Learn about this great practice later in the chapter.)

4. Once you've looked at all these components, set your plan for your curriculum connections and instructional connections you'll make during the week.

Make Calendar Connections

1. Look closely at the calendar again. Look at what this picture represents for students and teachers. This time, focus on the schedule and timing. Make it a weekly habit to pay close attention to what you are asking of your students for the week.
   - Keep an eye on your students' workload.
   - Pay attention to the complexity (both for time needed and for "brain-load") of different requirements or tasks.
   - Notice other big-school events that may take student time or energy.
   - Ask yourselves if the schedule you've outlined is reasonable.
2. Make adjustments where needed. Aim for manageable learning schedules for your students.
3. You may make team guidelines for managing reasonable schedules. For example, you might limit the number of total tests or quizzes each week, decide how many large projects students should have going at once, set homework schedules that rotate a day off for each subject area, or allow students time off from homework between large projects. As time goes along, get student input on this!
4. Be open to projects that require calendar variations to accommodate unique circumstances! I've seen a great strategy that teams use to bring all hands on deck for a special project in one of the subject areas. It takes creative use of class time and needs to be a priority for the week's calendar; it results in a great learning experience for students. We can call it the "Chopped-Clock Block." (a theme borrowed from the *Food Network TV Show, "Chopped."*) Here's how it works:

   The team takes a block of its core time in one day—the total time the team would spend in the core classes in the entire day. (This might give as much as four or more hours.) All that time is scheduled for students to finish a big project they've been assigned for one of the courses. For example, the Social

Studies assignment may be to create the written content for a website that features a country each student has chosen. In the Social Studies class, students have been gathering information about the country's geography, history, structure, and attractions.

The team dedicates the day to the task of getting the projects finished. All teachers dig in and work energetically to see that every student on the team gets the project done. Each of the teachers can lend their special expertise to the process. Sometimes teams bring in parent or caregiver volunteers or students from upper grades. The inspiration and challenge are to "beat the clock!" Like the clock on *Chopped*, the time counts down. A timekeeper will stop the clock when students need to go to PE or lunch or take other breaks. But all the core time focuses on the one goal. This process enables a teacher to gather a small group of students who may not respond well to the pressure of the clock to give individual assistance or to adapt the project for those students.

The atmosphere is dynamic. Students are motivated. And the grand reward is this: With this strategy, 100% of the students complete the project!

Set 10-Day Learning Goals for the Whole Team

We all have the data about what some students may continually struggle to master. I am sure any school district can burp up a binder full of the test scores and data needed to prove that. ***For example, some of our students still don't start a sentence with a capital and end with punctuation. Or, data may show that many still struggle with basic math facts.*** A great way to overcome glaring academic gaps is to have everyone on the team work on those needed skills. I've seen great success in rectifying sticky lapses in important skills with the use of 10-Day Learning Goals.

What is the source for these goals? They can flow from or be related to the common needs you see on your team calendar when you correlate the curriculum and instruction. Or they can be evident needs from your data reviews (see *The Successful Middle School Schedule,*[19] a companion guide to *The Successful Middle School: This We Believe,* from AMLE for more on conducting holistic data reviews). Or they can be goals that are just downright obvious from living and working with your students. Any of these reasons for 10-Day goals are fine! The bottom line: Replacing deficiencies with proficiencies improves kids' performances on a multitude of topics and tasks, in **all** subject areas. It gives kids a lot of confidence, too. ***And it spares teachers from many (more) gray hairs.*** It also saves teachers a lot of time wasted trying to teach more advanced concepts to kids who don't know the fundamentals.

Just imagine a team creating a list of areas where each teacher on the team can apply, include, and integrate some skills that would go a long way to reducing students' academic struggles!

For example, we could set this as one of our 10-Day Learning Goals: Everyone will use proper sentence structure for the next 10 days. Every item will start with a capital letter and end with the proper punctuation. The sentence will express a complete thought, and have a subject and predicate. "Everyone" means all students in every core class. In the past, some teachers might have said they are not worried if the student uses proper writing in a Social Studies or Math course. Well, for the next 10 days everyone will support proper sentence structure! The hope is that, after 10 days, more students will have increased and applied their knowledge about sentences—and correct sentences will be the norm.

The idea is for the team to set the goals together. The team can create a list from which to draw the 10 goals. This list can include basic academic tasks, organizational skills, social skills, and aspects of being a good human being. It won't be hard to keep adding to this list. Hopefully you'll also be able to check some off as they become habits for the students. By the way, curriculum directors love this because we are talking here about gaps our students might have in subject areas. And I love this because you can also have 10-Day Learning Goals for behavior.

Here's how it works:

- Teams choose one goal for a 10-day stretch. ***(Yep, this means a 10-Day Goal for every two weeks throughout the year.)*** It can be an academic or nonacademic goal. You can choose one academic goal and one nonacademic goal for the 10 days, but don't do more than one of either kind. You can use Resource #25, "10-Day Learning Goals" on page 215 for planning and reflecting on your goals.

- Teachers model and hold students to the goal, demonstrating the skill or process correctly for 10 straight days. **Okay, team members, read that again. Everyone on the team is demonstrating the goal's skill or behavior—this means everyone! You included!**

Here are some sample goals:

10 Day Learning Goals, Academic

Think about skills, procedures, or processes that can be taught or generalized to—and are useful in learning for—all the subject areas.

- Basic math facts
- Read (or make) a graph
- Read (or make) a table or chart
- Find and understand the meaning of a new word
- Select a group of five academic vocabulary terms useful in all content areas
- Essay structure
- Take notes
- Thinking skills (deduction, synthesis, predicting, concluding, etc.)
- Problem-solving steps
- Write a hypothesis
- Prepare (and give) a speech
- Respond to someone else's speech
- Write a proper, coherent paragraph
- Find main ideas
- Find a source
- Tell if a source is reliable and how you know
- Find evidence in a text, speech, or video to support a main idea
- Summarize a paragraph, story, article, or video (*Try this in 25 words or less!*)
- Follow steps for an inquiry

10 Day Learning Goals, Nonacademic

Think about reinforcing some of the common daily activities, as well as behaviors, attitudes, and sociable components of classroom and school life.

- Use "Please" and "Thank You"
- Look at people when you talk to them
- Use a student planner
- Keep track of assignments
- Get to class on time
- Show appropriate hallway behavior
- How to talk to peers
- How to use your locker
- How to organize a backpack
- How to get and use a hall pass
- Basic manners of various kinds (i.e., cell-phone manners)

Again, there are so many options.

Continue and Polish the Connections

With good planning and adequate team-meeting time dedicated to connecting curriculum, your team will grow into this wonderful habit. You'll love watching students flourish from the good teaching, deeper learning, and manageable schedules. And the more you do this, the better your team will be at it. So, once you've got the weekly process down,

- Be adventuresome and map out a whole month. Place the curriculum for each subject area on the wall and see what topics overlap. In many cases, we are spinning wheels re-teaching a topic, or repeatedly doing the same basic activity in different classes. And then we wonder why our students are bored. *That is why, when I am Ruler of Education, no child will ever graph M & M's after third grade.*
- Take a few minutes each quarter to talk about areas in which students are struggling. For example, if you know your students are not doing well with fractions, spend time as a team learning how to use fractions skills in all classes. This may be a struggle for some teachers who do not feel proficient in math or fractions. However, it can be done just by using common language. "Hey, class. We just read a short story that had two characters in conflict for half of the story and two more characters in conflict for another third

of the story. What fraction of the story did not include any conflict among these characters?" **OR**, "Did you notice that one-fourth of the characters were involved in some sort of conflict, and one-half of those were from the same family?" Add some visual math to other subjects; this is a helpful skill for math and other concepts. It won't hurt anyone in Language Arts class to put their math skills to work for a few minutes. ***It's not just Language Arts teachers who may balk at the idea of working on a math goal. Many Math teachers can't revert to previous aspects of the math curriculum either. They feel a constant pressure to keep moving forward.***

- Take the opportunity each quarter, also, to reflect on how your curriculum, instruction, and calendar connections are working. Reflect on your team process for this. Ask students to notice and share the connections. They might be surprised at what ideas and skills they've used in all the classes. You might be, too!

AVOID THESE ACTIONS

In this chapter, you've read about what to do to put Element 13 into action. Here's a quick list of some things **not** to do.

As you **work to form meaningful connections in curriculum and instruction,** steer clear of

1. Choosing or continuing instructional strategies without some evidence that they have positive effects on student success.
2. Neglecting to reinforce any connecting skills or concepts once the team has worked on them.
3. Forgetting to let kids suggest 10-Day Goals, particularly the non-academic goals.
4. Letting teachers get away with not meeting the 10-Day Goals themselves or without demonstrating the use of curriculum connections in content and skills.

ELEMENT 14

Document Everything!

The Successful Middle School: This We Believe
Characteristic Cross-Over

- The school engages families as valued partners.

G**reat teams** take care to keep an organized system of important communication actions and decisions.

WHY THIS ELEMENT IS ESSENTIAL

When teams have records of their contacts and all other important actions and documents related to students or teamwork, the entire school community benefits.

Here's what I see in schools where this element is done well:

- Teams aren't digging through piles of disconnected notes, lists, and logs to find information about a parent or caregiver concern, an intervention planned for a student, or a plan for an upcoming team celebration.
- It only takes minutes for the team to retrieve a family's phone number or a record of decisions made at a particular team meeting.
- When a discipline matter arises, teachers have a record of the student's history with concerns, referrals, interventions, and outcomes rather than having to recreate the details, calls, strategies, and results from memory.
- There's never a doubt as to what happened at a team meeting or what was said to a parent or caregiver on a phone call.

- When teachers talk to parents and caregivers, they already know everything that was written or discussed before this call.
- Leaders have access to an at-a-glance review of all the incidents, discussions, and decisions related to a particular student.

HOW TO PUT THIS ELEMENT INTO ACTION

These days, educators have several different grade book programs that districts have purchased for large sums of money. These programs help teacher analyze academic data, and are helpful to students and their families. They also allow teachers to enter grades and help everyone access lists of students who are missing work and assignments.

Yet, there are still individual teachers on a team who each keep a separate phone log when they call parents or caregivers (if any record is kept at all). Many team members keep separate notes on team meetings, separate lists for student of the week, separate information on student behavior contracts or academic interventions underway, or separate records of meetings with parents or caregivers and students. This can lead to massive disorganization. It also impedes good communication about a student's progress or issues. Multiple records and notes in multiple files can be especially problematic when a family member or an administrator asks about individual student information—when you need a coherent history on an issue.

Teachers on teams need to have **one place** to gather and access all student information that is not related to grades and missing assignments.

Keep Individual Student Folders

Great teams have a central location and system for keeping track of all communications related to their students. They collect student records and data in a folder for each student on the team. All teachers on the team have access to the folder and can use to see such information as:

How many times teachers have made positive or negative calls to the student's parents or caregivers (and what the topics and outcomes of the calls were).

If (and when) the student has been brought into a team meeting for a conference.
What the team discussed with the student at a meeting (and what was decided).
What academic or behavioral interventions are underway for the student.
If and when parents or caregivers have made inquiries to a teacher. **(This does not include if the inquiry is to ask whether page 54 was due yesterday!)**
How many times parents or caregivers have attended a conference during the year.
Contacts the team has had with support staff about a particular student.
Notes on information or discussions with the student's teachers outside the team.

As a team, make a list of contents for your student folders. These are the kinds of things to collect for records of your connections and actions with and about individual students:

- Family contact information—phone, address, and email
- Copies of texts or emails to and from parents or caregivers
- Texts or emails to and from teachers or the team (other than from parents or caregivers)
- Records of and notes from meetings or phone calls with parents or caregivers
- Notes from meetings with a student
- Academic interventions that have been designed by the team
- Behavioral interventions that have been designed by the team (TIPS plans)
- Discipline referrals
- Any other information important to the team about the student
- Samples of student work (if you are going to present that information at a meeting with a parent or caregiver)

A major component of keeping up your student folders will be logging communications of all kinds. Keep track of pertinent details. Create a manual or electronic spreadsheet (Google Doc works well) where you can do this in a consistent and speedy manner. Here's an example:

Spreadsheet for Contact Log (Student-Related Contacts)

Student	Advocate	IEP/504						
Date	Type of Contact	Person Making Contact	Person Contacted	Reason for Contact	Outcome	Follow-up	Rewards	Other

Student folders enable team members to see all student-related communications and outcomes that have occurred through the current year. If an administrator or counselor needs some of this background information, teams can share the folder.

The hardest part of this (or any centralized system) is maintaining it. That's why great teams always spend the first five minutes of a team meeting entering information into their logs. Many teams opt for a Google Drive folder for each student. This is free and allows users to create and change documents online. Teams find it to be a great way to maintain student folders. Here are some advantages of using this tool:

- It's easy to use.
- Everyone on the team can contribute to and update the same document.
- Multiple teachers can work on a student file at the same time.
- All information is in one location.
- Administrators can access all student files.
- Other teachers or support staff can access information if they are invited by the team to do so.

If you use Google Docs or Sheets, be sure to create a template prior to creating the electronic file for each student. This will solve the problem of going back and creating a new document for each student.

Google Docs is one choice of many. You may need to talk with your IT Director regarding the use of a system that is not attached to the district server.

The overall goal of any filing or storage system is to have one central location for student contact and information. It is crazy for every teacher on a team to keep a different record. To help influence change, teams need to have this kind of information organized and readily accessible. It's critical that teachers, teams, and administrators see a complete picture on a student and that teams can provide accurate data when dealing with a student. ***Whether the gathering place for student information is a file folder or an electronic document, it must be easily accessible by the whole team.***

Treat Student Folders as Confidential

Think about who needs to contribute to or have access to student folders—wherever they may be stored. It might be helpful to add an administrator, counselor, and the essentials teachers to the list. If the student is on an IEP, there may be a special education teacher or other specialists who legitimately need access.

But, be picky about this! The fewer people involved, the better. Even though these are not the sacred "student permanent record files," most of the items include confidential information.

Every team member must understand that these records are private and need to be handled according to all the rules of the school and state and federal government regarding student privacy and confidentiality. Don't leave files open on a laptop where any passerby can take a look. Don't leave paper copies of notes or records unattended. Handle and protect them thoughtfully. Remember that you can always make copies of a piece of the folder that is relevant to a matter concerning other personnel, sidestepping the need to give too many people full access.

Think of each of these folders or files as a kind of "student personal data file." They contain a lot of vital information about the person in their "job" as a student, serving as a blueprint to build a comprehensive plan that helps them to do their job best! And in the worst-case scenario, the data you collect can be used for a student expulsion hearing or court case.

Keep Team Records

There are many team matters that need to be documented, beyond those that have to do with individual students. This includes team actions and decisions, as well as any general documents the team creates. Believe me—you will be glad that you have paper or digital proof of what you've done, who you've consulted about a matter, and what the outcomes were. A record of these things is a great backup for your team's collective cluttered mind or possible forgetfulness. Such documentation will also serve you well—many times—when you're in a position of having to substantiate your actions to someone else ***(such as an administrator, parent, or caregiver—or, trust me, it might even be a fellow teammate who says, "No, that is not what we decided!")***.

Keep all records in one location, central enough for the whole team to easily access: in an online program such as Google Docs or in old-fashioned, hard copy format.

Here are things a great team records:

- Records and notes on all contacts with support staff in relation to team matters
- All team-meeting agendas
- All team-meeting minutes (Make these thorough to begin with, and it will save lots of hassles later!)
- Team decisions
- Procedures and policies the team creates
- Agendas for all-team meetings (with students)
- Notes on follow-up to any all-team meetings
- Overall look at team's 10-Day Learning Goals
- Overview of team's PD goals and activities
- List of strategies for discipline interventions
- List of strategies for academic interventions
- Summaries (and dates) of communications with other teams
- Copies of forms, such as those you create for planning, letters sent to all parents, notices of team events, etc.

You get the idea! As you do this, your team will come to realize what needs to be kept in this collection.

For an efficient way to keep track of the communications within or outside the team, create a spread sheet similar to the one you use for contacts about students.

Set up a table of contents or some way to organize the items in categories for easy retrieval. As with the communications records kept in individual student folders, this common collection of team business matters will save hours of searching ***and probably many expletives that you'd not allow from students.***

Be Consistent

Record-keeping and documentation are the easiest things to avoid or delay. It's almost natural to think, "We'll do that later." There are so many times that you will need to be able to put your hands—quickly—on any number of things listed in this chapter. The few minutes you spend putting a form into a folder or dropping a PDF of a note from a parent into your Google Doc will be well worth the effort. Do this conscientiously, consistently, and promptly. Dedicate the first five minutes of every team meeting to entering this information into the communication log.

AVOID THESE ACTIONS

In this chapter, you've read about what to do to put Element 14 into action. Here's a quick list of some things **not** to do.

As you **create student and team folders to document all important things,** steer clear of

1. Being careless with any of the documentation, particularly that which is related to individual students.
2. Sharing information in student files or team folders outside the team (or to anyone not specifically involved in a student matter). This includes sharing verbally.
3. Forgetting to date every item you add to a student or team folder.
4. Failing to organize the student or team files so that you can find what is in them.
5. Procrastinating with documentation or skipping it altogether.

ELEMENT 15

Fit In with the Rest of the School

The Successful Middle School: This We Believe
Characteristic Cross-Over

- A shared vision developed by all stakeholders guides every decision.
- The school engages families as valued partners.

Great teams intentionally form and sustain harmonious, productive integration with the overall school program and the people in it.

WHY THIS ELEMENT IS ESSENTIAL

Everyone in the school community benefits when teams have strong, consistent communication and interconnection with other teams, school staff members, and students' families.

Here's what I see in schools where this element is done well:

- Teams don't compete with each other. They uphold each other and share ideas.
- Teams are happy for the input, challenges, and camaraderie provided in their connections outside of the team.
- Teams are stronger and better at their jobs because they embrace outside support.
- Teachers are not cliquey; they build strong professional connections with other adults throughout the school.

- Students are loyal to their teams but not dismissive of other teams or of experiences outside the team. They enjoy important connections and positive influences from adults outside the team.
- Parents and caregivers feel good about the school. They know what's going on. They feel included. And they know they have partners in working for their child's success.
- Leaders don't have to go scrounging for updates and information from teams. They love the open flow of communication.

HOW TO PUT THIS ELEMENT INTO ACTION

Previous elements of effective teaming in this book address the value of team identity and unity. Yes, that's super important. But no team is an island! Teams aren't and shouldn't operate as if their group is on its own. Quite frankly, some teams become competitive with one another; the teaming process turns into a running contest of which team is the sharpest, most successful, or most fun to belong to.

Great teams know that their success is intertwined with the grander support system around them. They realize that they are at their best for the welfare of the students (and teachers) when they purposely function as part of the wider teaming culture—made up of everybody pulling together to create outstanding learning experiences for all students.

It's both satisfying and productive for teams to make intentional, frequent connections with others in the school community—to support and receive support from a number of other parties. Teams must put the cultivation of outside-the-team contacts and relationships on their goal lists and planning schedules. These are as sacred as good relationships within the team. When these connections are **not** a priority, all kinds of mix-ups, misunderstandings, and missed opportunities occur. Your students will not get the best possible academic experiences or the overall personal, emotional, and social support they deserve.

Value the energy, expertise, and gifts that are available to your team from many sources. Here are some strategies and bits of advice for where to find those gifts and how to thrive from working with others who care about students as much as you do.

Make Connections with Essentials Teachers

Most middle schools have essentials classes (aka *electives* or *exploratory classes*) as part of the program for all students. In some schools, essentials teachers teach large numbers of students from multiple teams; they might see twice as many students a week as the regular team. Sometimes an essentials teacher is part of a core team. And, as I described in Element 3 where I discussed creating teams, some schools have teams of essentials teachers. Whatever your school's teaming structure, essentials teachers can be great assets in addressing student concerns and advocating for students. Open communication between teams and essentials teachers leads to marvelous opportunities for cross-curricular instruction and deeper understandings of early adolescent development for all the teachers involved.

Connections Ideas:

- Note: Because students choose areas of their personal interest or talents for essentials classes, they sometimes form uniquely strong bonds with an essentials teacher. These teachers can provide the core team with valuable insights about the child. The team, in return, can provide insights to the essentials teacher that will strengthen the student's success in the essentials class.
- Communication is one of the toughest issues surrounding the connections between core teams and essentials teachers. In many cases, core teams feel that they are keeping the essentials teachers in the loop, while the essentials teachers feel they are the last to know about things within the team. Close this gap with planned strategies for communicating.
- See that every team has a designated "essentials-communicator." This person informs the essentials teachers about student needs, issues, and team logistics that are pertinent to the essentials classes. If the essentials teachers in the school also have a team, their team needs a communicator, too, to keep contact with the core teams. The communicators from the core and essentials teams share such information as
    - ◇ Student needs, issues, or concerns that they see in their classes
    - ◇ Interventions underway for a student

- ◇ Schedules and other logistics
- ◇ Overview of current content being taught in the essentials class or on the team
- ◇ Description of major projects currently underway

- Plan some team-meeting time on a regular basis (maybe monthly) to meet with the essentials teachers (or representative of the essentials team) to discuss kids, curriculum, and professional development. This lets essentials teachers know that the core team sees them as critical to the teaming process and values what they can learn from the essentials teachers. This communication becomes an effective mutual-support system.
- We all need to be reminded of this: **essentials classes** are what bring a good number of young adolescent students to school. ***As my good friend and avid middle school advocate Kathy Hunt Ullock always said, "Let's face it: for many kids, the worst part of the apple is the CORE."*** Knowing this, great teams give ongoing, enthusiastic support to these teachers. Teams work closely with essentials teachers (or essentials teams) to suggest and devise new essentials classes. Together, they solicit student ideas for essentials classes that students would like as options.
- Essentials teams can plan an "E-Event" where they invite students and families to experience the highlights of learning that takes place in their essentials classes. For example, an arts teacher could have demonstrations of molding clay. The band teacher could have small groups of students practicing their instruments to show how students work together to learn the notes and the skills of producing music. The theater teacher could hold a short drama-skills tutorial giving visitors pointers on how to read a script, project voices, or move about the stage. The home economics demonstration could involve visitors in making taffy or sewing a cool patch on their jeans. So often when we showcase a course or advertise an essentials topic, we show finished products. The idea here is that the "E-Event" instead gives students an idea of the learning processes for these classes—and maybe even draws them into a learning process for 10 or 15 minutes.

Make Connections with Other Teachers and Support Staff

Numerous other members of the school staff lend support to your team and to each of your students. There are many good times and reasons to nurture communication with these folks. In some cases, this will require meetings, discussions, or joint planning. In others, the connection is a matter of acknowledgement and short communications. Here are some of the people to notice, value, and engage with where you can. They all affect the well-being of your team and your students.

P.E., music, and arts teachers
Special ed teachers
Foreign language teachers
Reading specialists
Counselors
Media specialists
Paraprofessionals
Custodians
Office staff
Social workers
Bus drivers
Psychologists
Nurses
Nutritionists and food service workers
Administrators
Curriculum directors
Tech and data specialists
Behavior specialists
Virtual teaching coordinators
IP coordinators
Family liaisons

Never overlook the truth that the bus driver, custodian, secretary, or lunchroom supervisor may have an incredibly meaningful connection with a student on your team, and they may notice a student's needs or talents that no one on the team sees.

Connections Ideas:

- Try this: As a team, make a list of the staff members in your school. You could do this with individual names or with job categories. A few times each year (maybe quarterly) take some team-meeting time to look through the list together. Share about a time or subject on which someone on the team has made a connection of any sort with the person(s). Keep notes to remind yourselves of how you might acknowledge, support, or learn something from each of these people—especially those who you've hardly noticed. You might check off names as you make contacts. This is particularly helpful when you work in a large school.

- Make a point to take advantage of insights or support some of these other staff members can give to your team. Ask for their ideas, opinions, or advice. Show appreciation for their professional skills and their important contributions to your students.
- For others who don't have obvious interaction with one or more of your students as a part of their jobs, intentionally initiate casual contacts: Give a word of gratitude or encouragement; share a funny story; give a helping hand for a few minutes; let the person know how they're helpful to you; notice how a person has influenced one (or more) or your students—and tell the person. When you put the importance of these connections on your radar, the sense of pride, respect, professionalism, and value soars for your team and these other folks. As a team, you might send them a card thanking them for something specific they did for your team. For example, if the curriculum director provided some great resources for your team, send a card telling them how that helped.

Make Connections with Other Teams and Grade Levels

Teams need each other. A spirit of friendly competition doesn't hurt—but make your relationships with other teams primarily about mutual support and goals for kids. Teams and students benefit from all kinds of connections among teams. Here are a few ideas; teams will think of many more. Students can contribute ideas too!

Connections Ideas:

- Share successful strategies and team practices—for curriculum connections, great instruction, team-meeting processes, discipline, scheduling, classroom management, stress-reduction, relationships with kids, student voice, and a host of other things!
- Inform each other about big projects, schedule changes that might affect the other teams, or plans to launch rockets outside the other team's windows or turn the nearby hallway into a stage for your team's upcoming dance contest.
- Now and then, plan a joint activity with another team or with all the grade-level teams. Think about combining forces for a fundraiser, playground clean-up hour, fun contest, project show-off time, or art walk.

- Join the teachers from another team for a professional development activity. Practice an innovative teaching strategy, read and discuss a great article or video, or perfect a team process.

Make Connections with Students' Families

Most likely, your team has already planned to start off the year with welcoming contacts to parents and caregivers. In previous elements I've discussed several strategies for informing families about (and inviting their participation in) team mission statements, team policies and procedures, discipline processes, and regular communications about their child's academic work and overall school success.

But as the school year continues, stay alert for ways to continue caring for relationships with families. We all know that the relationships we build with parents and caregivers make a huge difference in any student's success. Remember that families have a need to belong to the school, just as the students do. Positive connections increase a family's sense of connection to the school, and they heighten the chances that parents and caregivers will support the school (and the teachers and the team), stay involved, trust the teachers and the school, and support you in any interventions you'll need to plan for their child. All this translates to greater success for the child.

Connection Ideas:

- **Quick, in-person contacts.** I know there are perhaps fewer small, casual contacts these days, due to concerns about viruses and school safety. Parents or caregivers can't just walk in, as in the "olden days." Nevertheless, you're likely to catch glimpses of a family member on some occasions, such as when they drop off a kid in the parking lot or attend a PTA meeting or other school event. ***(This contact may even happen at the Dollar Store or when you go to get a root canal, or when you pick up your antidepressants prescription at the pharmacy.)*** Take the opportunity to wave, say "Hi" or "Welcome," wish them well, or quickly mention something that you love about their child.
- **Regular written or phone contacts.** Some teams plan for each student's family to get a brief note or message from one of the team teachers at various

times. This can be a written, mailed postcard, a text, a call, or an email. Make sure these are positive messages—about a kind or helpful gesture that the child did for someone else, something you are impressed or excited about, a characteristic of the student that you enjoy, or an accomplishment. Find ways to let parents or caregivers know that you believe that their child can succeed.

- **Reliable flow of information.** A major goal of connections with families is letting them know what is happening. Share calendar events, team data (appropriate to share with public), team accomplishments, and important parts of the schedule. Let them know what the expectations are for their children, how the children are to meet them, and that the team will work hard to help them meet the expectations. A lot of important messages can be shared by posting essential information and the team calendar on the website or through the parent portal, and with text, emails, or written reminders. Hopefully, at the beginning of the school year, your team has asked families about the best ways to communicate with each one. Not all families have Internet or digital devices. Be sure the team has identified a reliable way to get team information to each family. Also, take care to provide any written or phone messages in a language that the family member can understand.
- **Expressions of gratitude.** Look for every opportunity to show your appreciation to a family member for what they do for the child, and for what they contribute to helping you or the school processes. It only takes a few words. Use the word "grateful" frequently. Be specific about their act or words that inspired your gratitude.
- **Team events that include families.** Develop intentional activities that involve parents, caregivers, and other family members. These can extend to events beyond the once-a-year Fall Open House or the student conferences. Families can join in a bingo night, team poetry slam, talent show, all-team birthday celebration, game hour, pizza party, or may other events workable for including families. These might be held on the playground or field, or in the gym or auditorium.
- **Lessons to learn from families.** Invite parents or caregivers to contribute knowledge, skills, or experiences with your students. This can be done

through video chats with the class or small groups. The family members can share about their careers, hobbies, or anything else they know about or know how to do. It's a super way for parents and caregivers, or even siblings, to contribute to learning experiences for your students.

- **Invitations for their insights.** Yes, you spend a lot of time with the students on your team and work to get to know them as individuals. You talk with them and about them, follow their progress, address their needs. But parents or caregivers know the rest of the story—and the history. Your bond with students is strong, but theirs is usually far stronger. Ask them for their insights and advice. Learn about the student from them. Listen to their input. Some of these contacts can be done via FaceTime or Zoom. Make use of what you learn from these family contacts. Give them feedback about what you did with the information they shared. This lets them know that you are a true co-advocate for their child. It's a powerful way to increase the bond with families.
- **Support of student interests.** Attend extracurricular events to support students on your team. When you support a student by attending a performance, sporting event, club demonstration or celebration, concert, science fair, art exhibition, debate competition, or any other venue in which the student participates, you give a strong message of connection and caring to the student and the family. ***And hey, being there when a student helps out at a community food bank, sells their prize-winning heifer, plays softball, competes in a swim meet, or sings in the choir is also a fun experience for you! Bring your own children along!***
  Your message of support is meaningful, even if the only contact you have is a smile, a wave across the bleachers, a loud whistle, or a boisterous "Go, Chantel!!" shouted to the player. ***Note: Even if the parent or caregiver was not present at the event and thus, did not actually witness your attendance and enthusiasm—they will hear about it! And the connection is still made.***
- **Respectful communications.** Keep all contacts kind. Be sure your communications, attitudes, and nonverbal communication are genuine, caring, and bias free. Let parents and caregivers know that you have high regard for them—that they matter.

Follow These Tips for All Communications

- Keep records; use your team communication log, team folder, or team Google Doc or other digital record to note any contacts that include information or outcomes the team will need to remember or document. (See Element 14 for more documentation suggestions.)
- This bears repeating from Element 14: Honor the confidentiality of communications. Be careful to keep written communications in a secure place, particularly when sharing information about student issues, performance, or behavior.
- No matter who the parties involved in team communications may be, know this: **Your students are watching and listening** ***(Yes, even if they act like they have no interest in anything you do or say)***. They notice how you treat each other; they particularly notice how you relate to their families. They need to see that their parents, caregivers, and siblings are included, respected, helped, and informed equally to the families of other students. Observing such connections enhances their comfort, sense of belonging, and trusting bond with the team.

AVOID THESE ACTIONS

In this chapter, you've read about what to do to put Element 15 into action. Here's a quick list of some things **not** to do.

As you plan **ways to connect with members of the school community outside your team**, steer clear of

1. Taking any actions or making any comments that undermine, demean, stereotype, or gossip about other staff members or students' family members.
2. Tolerating attitudes or behaviors that characterize parents or caregivers, other teams, administrators, or any staff members, as "the enemy."
3. Failing to interact in a manner that shows equal regard for all the persons with whom you make connections.
4. Repeating communications (outside the team) that are meant to be private exchanges between the team and another person or group.

5. Leaving the connections to chance—without intentionally making them.
6. Starting off strong then letting this commitment slide.

ELEMENT 16

Never Stop Learning and Growing

The Successful Middle School: This We Believe
Characteristic Cross-Over

- Professional learning for all staff is relevant, long term, and job embedded.

Great teams take charge of their own professional development. They find time and ways to evaluate their teaming processes and offer each other stimulating opportunities for learning and growing together.

WHY THIS ELEMENT IS ESSENTIAL

When teams deliberately engage in learning with each other to improve their teaming and teaching practices, it is not only the teachers who benefit. Their growth is a boon to all their students and the school community beyond their classrooms.

Here's what I see in schools where this element is done well:

- The team's honest self-evaluations lead to better teaming. Team members build even greater trust and better working relationships as they collectively reflect on their accomplishments and future goals.
- Teachers find satisfaction in what they learn. They're more excited about what they teach. They are more confident and creative, and take risks to try new things. Morale and job satisfaction are high for the team members.
- Teams are eager to share what they learn with other teams. They don't compete with other teams, but uphold each other and share ideas.

- Other teams pick up good habits from the teams that do professional development effectively.
- Kids learn and achieve more. Both students and their families benefit from the enriched understanding of students, more engaging classrooms, and heightened teaching abilities.
- Leaders are relieved of some of the professional development planning. Also, leaders learn things as teams share what they learn with others.

HOW TO PUT THIS ELEMENT INTO ACTION

An effective team is one of the best models of a professional learning community that I know. Unfortunately, we (the adults on the team) don't think of ourselves as the learners—at least not often enough. When I step into a school to work with teams, the teachers are not surprised to hear me talk about a focus on kids or a focus on curriculum. They expect this. But most teams have not thought of their cooperative teaching group as a professional development unit, with their own growth and development as a goal. So, I will get on my soap box again: "Hey, everyone! A great team sees the team and everyone on it as an amazing resource for professional development!"

Yes, you will grow and develop and learn and teach better—just by being a part of an effective team. But your team will be so much more mature and effective IF you consciously plan for new learning experiences within your team.

Reflect—Frequently and Fearlessly

Team reflection is a cornerstone of good professional development. It is, in itself, a growth process. And the things you learn from honestly looking at where you are as a team, what you've done, and where your strengths and challenges lie, inform many of your future professional development goals. That's why great teams take some of their PD time to examine and evaluate their effectiveness. They ask the tough questions, accept the shortfalls and concerns, delight in the accomplishments, and maybe even have to drive through "Uglyville" to get to "Great."

Here are some ideas for approaching the task of team reflection and evaluation:

Start with a light-hearted reflection. Introduce the topic of team evaluation with a humorous survey such as Resource #26, "Some Reflections on Our Team." You'll find it on pages 216-217.

This tongue-in-cheek activity can help you ask each other the hard questions. Sometimes humor helps take the edge off the realities we need to notice and accept. This casual "survey" is fun, but it raises important questions.

Work together to answer these questions honestly. Don't approach any of these with shame or blame. Doing this activity together will help your team identify strengths. It will help you see where and how you spend your team time. It will remind you about the good work your team must do—far beyond spending huge amounts of time talking about students (much of it unproductively). It will remind you that when teams do use their time in some of the ways reflected in the answer choices, other important teamwork— academic achievement for all students, curriculum connections, teacher morale, and professional growth— never gets discussed.

Ask some simple questions. How do you know if your team needs to make some changes? Start by simply asking these questions:

1. *Do we spend 95% of our time on the same 5% of our kids?*
2. *Are we far from fulfilling our team goals or mission?*
3. *Are we using terms such as "these kids" or "those kids"?*
4. *Does one person control our team time?*
5. *Do we tend to focus on one team member who is not being a team player?*
6. *Are there days when any of us crave the feeling of being a teacher in a one-room schoolhouse?*
7. *Have we increased our knowledge of adolescent development?*
8. *Are we up to date on pop culture trends and societal changes?*

If you answered *yes* to several of these questions, take a few minutes during your next team meeting to discuss what the answers have shown you about your team. This will guide you to some professional development needs and goals.

Use a teaming evaluation form. For a more extensive look at teaming effectiveness, you could create a casual checklist for yourselves, itemizing the elements of teaming that you've tackled. Or, for a more thorough evaluation, make use of AMLE's Successful Middle School Assessment tools. Find more information at amle.org/sms.

However you go about your evaluation, once you identify elements of teaming or parts of elements that you have well in hand, others areas where you've made progress, and areas that need more work, you'll have greater insights into how to spend your team meeting time. As well, your team will gain direction for the PD topics and activities you want to pursue.

Invite feedback from outside the team. There are people in the school community besides your teammates who know some things about your team's effectiveness. If you're brave enough, solicit input from students, colleagues outside of your teammates, administrators, and students' parents and caregivers. This may feel too time consuming, but you will gain valuable insights from all these sources. You could limit it to a simple question, such as: "What observations, ideas, or comments would you like to share about our team?" or "How is our team doing?"

Ask for student feedback. I strongly urge you, at the least, to solicit some sort of reflection from the students on your team. After all, aren't they the ones who know the most about how things are working? Design a brief survey to ask for their input on such topics as team unity, consistency with protocols, consistency with discipline, favorite curriculum connections, thoughts about team meetings, how the team helps them academically, ideas for celebrations, the best thing the team contributes to them, and suggestions they want to make. Better yet, turn the creation of the survey over to the kids.

When you do ask for and receive feedback from students or from anyone outside the team, make sure that you take it seriously and act on it. Those who took the time to thoughtfully respond need to see that you acted on their suggestions.

After you finish any kind of reflection or receive feedback from someone outside the team, don't drop it in a file and walk away. Identify items that are of concern—that need further discussion, a policy revision, more team time, more practice, or change. Put these on a team meeting agenda or PD activity menu for the future. Then, be sure to complete the same form or answer the same questions again in a few months. Celebrate your team's growth!

Make Team Professional Development a Priority

Commit to use a portion of your team time for activities that inform, stretch, deepen, and better yourselves as teachers and team members. Give yourselves the luxury of seeking learning opportunities together. You're all better when you challenge and support each other. Teams that deliberately engage in learning

- Become better at teaming.
- Become better teachers individually.
- Grow as persons.
- Learn more about students' current struggles and successes.
- Address all kinds of student needs and issues effectively.
- Delight in watching their students thrive.
- Set a wonderful model of adults as students who keep on learning.

During your very busy lives and schedules, teams must find ways to stimulate learning for themselves. Here are a few guidelines:

Think short. You do not have to plan exhaustive seminars or long meetings. If you're reading, watching, or listening to something together, start with short, engaging examples (even a headline, book title, quote, or cartoon). For longer pieces, break something into manageable segments. Each person can take a piece of an article, read and digest it, and share three take-away points with other teammates.

Think ahead. Stay alert for topics that could lend themselves to some PD. For instance, if you have a challenging decision that you cannot seem to make, investigate decision-making models. If a new standard or mandate comes your way, put it on your PD agenda and be ready to each bring one idea about implementing it to your next meeting. If a rough situation comes up over and over during your teaching, ask a teammate to videotape your class. An analysis and problem-solving session about the issue can be good PD. *Thinking ahead might even mean being aware of TikTok trends and other chaotic social media posts that cause us angst and frustrations.*

Think teammates. Look around your team. Remember that each person on your team is a great resource for professional development. When members share strategies, ideas, insights, or mistakes, every other person is enriched. If you are lucky to have an academic coach on your staff, ask them to provide some PD.

Think variety. There are dozens of ways to learn together. Think outside the box! Mix up the ways you learn—just as you mix up learning strategies for your students. Learn from articles, book chapters, videos, speeches, websites, blogs, and demonstrations. Learn from each other, collogues from outside the team, or members of the community. Host a focus group of parents and caregivers. Use students as teachers sometimes—they have a lot to teach you! Take field trips. Test out strategies or lessons on one another. Take turns presenting one idea each in a different modality: include music, movement, images, interviews, games, and many other approaches. For more ideas of PD topics and ways to learn together, see Resource #27, "Ideas for Team Professional Development," on page 218.

Think student concerns. Be sure to include the topics that involve and weigh on your students most. Take a deep-dive into such topics as social media, young adolescent trends, diversity issues, bias, and gender identity. Invite your students to present to the teachers some of their knowledge, opinions, and experiences on these topics (and other topics they believe you should hear about).

Think organization. Collect ideas for team professional development. Spend some time culling the ideas and identifying those you need most. Build these into a menu of things you will pursue. Make a timeline, scheduling topics once or twice a month for several months in advance. When you put something on the schedule, assign a person to facilitate an activity around that topic. Of course, you can always switch topics around if an urgent PD need arises. For an example of a planning form, see Resource #28, "Our Team PD Menu and Timeline," on page 219.

AVOID THESE ACTIONS

In this chapter, you've read about what to do to put Element 16 into action. Here's a quick list of some things **not** to do.

As you plan **team evaluation and professional development**, steer clear of

1. Learning a new strategy and never using it.
2. Taking on too much at once. (Really, you can learn and grow a lot as a team with short experiences.)
3. Avoiding topics that are challenging or uncomfortable (like bias, student mental health, or team dynamics).
4. Forgetting to acknowledge and celebrate the team's successful learning experiences and new skills gained.
5. Skipping the snacks at PD sessions. Remember, eating makes a meeting!

Stay Connected to the Power

Some Final Thoughts on Teaming

This book began with a message about the power of teaming. I leave the readers—teams working together, individual team members, and their supportive school communities—with a hearty appeal to take advantage of that power. I hope your eyes, ears, minds, and hearts will be fully open to the astounding possibilities offered by great teaming. I truly believe that quality teaming, implemented and sustained, meets so many of the needs of middle school students and reduces (or eliminates) so many of the usual frustrations.

I challenge every school to diligently develop and refine each of the essential teaming elements. And I challenge every team member to continue to grow as teams, and to continue to strengthen your own contributions to your team. Remember that effective teaming is not a destination; it is an ongoing endeavor—an awesome adventure of constant learning.

Plug into the power of teaming to keep going and growing. Here are important ways to continue your adventure:

Be grateful for your teaming opportunity: I've mentioned research that shows consistent, effective teaming practices raise the frequency of individual classrooms exhibiting best instructional practices —all of which lead to higher student achievement and better morale for teachers. Yes, it is exciting to see research confirm this. But it is even more thrilling to BE a part of a dynamic teaming process, working in a productive partnership with other teachers, as well as with students, administrators, and families, to generate the many amazing benefits for all involved. How satisfying it is to be smack in the middle of the work of building better relationships, following flashes of creativity to connect concepts and skills across content areas, boosting students' academic confidence while drastically reducing failures, designing realistic interventions that really work for kids, and helping to expand strong, visible advocacy for every student on the team!

Be courageous, and work hard for effective teaming: We educators who believe in teaming and work at it daily—we can do this! This means you. You can do this! Set your goals and expectations high. Know that every day of teaming makes each teacher stronger. Embrace the togetherness of the team; draw energy from it to build courage to try new ideas, solve problems, take risks, and care for your students. Be brave enough to have the tough conversations within the team and find solutions and answers. Enjoy the long-term sense of friendship and family that's possible to form with your teammates. Be grateful that you are a part of something grand beyond your own classroom. And to you administrators: trust and respect your teams. Give them the support and flexibility to solve problems and make decisions. Support their efforts to grow as a group and as persons and professionals. Make sure they know that YOU know that teaming is vital to the success of the school and every student in it. Let them see you energized, too, by teaming—and continually fighting for it.

Allow yourselves to be awed by your students: Our middle school students are amazing. Invite them to fully participate in the teaming process. Too often we forget to seek their knowledge, input, advice, and leadership. These young adolescents have a passion for change; they challenge the status quo. They do care about their future. They want to solve problems; and they have inventive ideas. They are hungry to talk about social issues and about the truths of their world. They have lived through the pandemic and, as students, have had a unique experience. They want to talk about what they endured and witnessed. They want to speak up on topics of human rights, the cruelty they witness through social media, and gender issues. They have opinions on individual freedoms, school violence, mass shootings, the benefits and consequences of technology, prejudice, harassment, mental health, and the environment. Listen to your students. Take time to notice how creative and inspiring they can be. Learn from them. They see the world from a perspective unlike that of adults. Appreciate this. **Your team will be strongest if you soak up what these awesome young people have to offer to you.**

Invite your students into the teaming processes: As a team, fully embrace student voices and provide as many opportunities as possible for them to make choices about what goes on within the team. Include students in making decisions about team-wide rules and expectations. They can demonstrate and teach these to fellow students. Students can make presentations in team meetings about topics of their interest. They can keep teachers up-to-date on the latest fashions, fads, trends, music, and slang. They can let you know what issues kids need to discuss. Students have great insights about how to involve their families in the teaming process. Just ask them! See that your great team lets students do more of the talking.

Value students' families: How to involve parents in middle schools, how to gain their support and assure their sense of belonging—these have long been big mysteries for the middle level grades. Families crave quality communication. They want to be welcomed and included. And when they see their children embraced by a team, they want to be part of the team, too. Yet, in many cases, kids don't even want a parent seen near them on the same city block—let alone actually walk into the school to drop off a forgotten lunch or book. The embarrassment is too much for the young adolescent! But great teams find ways to comfortably include parents in activities. They keep a constant flow of communication with frequent personal messages to individual families. They make sure that the positive, grateful, and congratulatory messages far outweigh the "concerns." Quality teams also provide ideas for parents and caregivers on helping to raise and live with young adolescents. Families want teachers to understand their community, their culture, their worries, and the perils and fears of raising a child in this world of social media and other challenges (and dangers). They don't want to be excluded, blamed, or shamed. They genuinely appreciate ideas and solutions. Teams are in a unique and wonderful position to embrace and help families.

Get students' families on your team: Okay, it's true that educators these days experience plenty of disrespect from students' families and the wider community. They experience families, often, as the opposition. Teams can make a major dent in this problem by showing families that the ideas about teachers are misconceptions.

By offering sincere and sustained regard for students' families (in all their configurations and personalities), teams can show how passionate teachers are about middle school kids, about helping their child succeed, and about teaching their child and everyone else's child on the team equally. By inviting families into the school processes and constantly informing them about the work of the team and the progress of their children, teams can demonstrate how hard teachers work to be creative, competent, and creative. Teams can help parents and caregivers understand how their partnership with the school is critical to encouraging good teachers to stay in the profession and provide excellent education. Again—recognize and fire up the power of the team! Your respect, kindness, and communication with families, along with your demonstration of how you are helping their children succeed, can reverse negativity and engender new appreciation for the teaching profession and the wonderful benefits of your middle school practices. The whole school community will benefit from a robust two-way advocacy between home and the school!

Treasure and protect the team and teaming: Teachers on a team want to have fun and enjoy teaching as they really make a difference in kids' lives. Teaming has the potential to provide a pleasant and stimulating environment for you as professionals. Don't be diverted from that by petty squabbles or gossip. Strive hard to accomplish important team tasks together—this is what makes everything work well! The best way to protect the **gift of teaming** and prolong its power for your students and your teaching is to use the team's common planning time so very, very wisely. That way, no one will ever be able to claim that teaming in your school is "just another planning period for the individual teachers!" Never take the chance of losing teaming in your school. Cherish the time you have to focus on kids, curriculum, and professional development. Enjoy the teaming journey. It is life-changing for you, your students' families, and the extraordinary young adolescents you teach.

Resource Pages

1. The 1-2-4 Process
2. Administrator's Checklist for Team Observation
3. Questionnaire 1, Getting to Know Your Teammates
4. Questionnaire 2, Do you Really know Your Teammates?
5. We Stand for This ... Team Panther
6. The Explorers We Believe:
7. Team Dynamite Vision
8. Where Are We Now? Page 1
   Where Are We Now? Page 2
9. Some Decision-Making Models
10. Anatomy of a Decision
11. Team Roles and Responsibilities
12. Some Team-Meeting Personalities
13. The Aviators Team Meeting Agenda
14. The Dolphins Team Meeting Agenda
15. The Comets Team Meeting Agenda
16. Examining Our Team's Current Expectations
17. Our Team Protocols
18. TIPS Planning Form
19. Looking at All the Factors That Affect Students
    Looking at All the Factors That Affect Students, Template

20. Ideas for TIPS Action Plans
21. The Index Card Activity
22. Thumbs Up, Thumbs Down
23. Academic Success Check, Team Record
24. Ways to Connect Curriculum
25. 10-Day learning Goals
26. Some Reflections on Our Team, Page 1
    Some Reflections on Our Team, Page 2
27. Ideas for Team Professional Development
28. Our Team PD Menu and Timeline

Resource #1

The 1 - 2 - 4 Process

Ways to Reach Agreement on Just About Anything

one

Individuals work alone to write their versions of the topic at hand (definition, description of how something will look, or a statement).

two

Each individual joins another person. The pair creates a version upon which they can both agree.

four

Two pairs join and create another version upon which they all agree.

whole group

All "fours" share their versions with the group. Together, the group creates a version that brings consensus out of all the two-pair visions.

Resource #2

Administrator's Checklist for Team Observation

Use this as a guide to note what you observe when you visit a team meeting—what you hear, watch in action, or see evidence of its existence and use.

	Priority Topics	Notes
	Discussion of student needs and progress	
	Curriculum and instruction connections	
	Sharing of instructional strategies	
	Professional development plans or activity	

	Meeting Logistics & Climate	Notes
	A visible, well-planned agenda	
	Followed the agenda	
	Full participation of all members	
	Collegial communication	
	Support staff consulted when needed	

	Support Strategies for Students	Notes
	3-5-7 academic checks	
	3-5-7 support strategies identified	
	TIPS process for discipline and other interventions	

	Team Calendar	Notes
	Student workload, assignments, tests	
	Homework	
	Dates for Weeks 3, 5, 7, Academic Checks	
	All-team events (students)	
	Scheduled team meetings	

	Contacts with Parents	Notes
	System for recording contacts with parents	
	Information entered into the communication log in the last week	
	Support strategies for students entered into parent contact log	
	Team-wide calls or notes to parents, caregivers	

	Team Rewards and Celebrations	Notes
	Team-wide rewards created	
	Team-wide celebrations planned	

Team ______________________ Date ______________

Resource #3

QUESTIONNAIRE 1

Getting to Know Your Teammates

Complete the questionnaire about yourself. Circle all of the choices that apply. You will be sharing your responses with your team. Find the response closest to the reality that seems to fit you.

1. My favorite cuisine is
a) Italian.
b) Sugar-based.
c) Meat and potatoes.
d) School lunch.

2. What makes me want to binge-watch TV is
a) Pure loneliness in the evenings.
b) Avoidance of grading papers.
c) The joy of actually finishing something.
d) To stay hip with the younger generation.

3. The car I drive is
a) Really cool
b) A hybrid
c) In the shop a lot
d) An unmarked car

4. If I weren't a teacher, I would be
a) A rodeo clown.
b) A travel agent.
c) A therapist.
d) In therapy.

5. For fun, I
a) Engage in athletic things, like running, volleyball, or weightlifting.
b) Read.
c) I don't do fun!
d) Roll my eyes at students.

6. The best thing(s) to smell at school is (are)
a) Markers.
b) Glue or rubber cement.
c) Kids' lockers.
d) Hand sanitizer.

7. My family thinks I am
a) In witness protection.
b) Totally cool.
c) A whiner.
d) A wiener.

8. I wish my family thought I were
a) In witness protection.
b) Totally cool.
c) Too fragile to have to work.
d) Needier than I let on.

9. When I relax, I like to wear
a) P.J.s.
b) As little as possible.
c) Sweats.
d) My favorite Halloween costume.

10. If I could run away for a week, I'd go to
a) A place with no cell service.
b) The beach.
c). The mountains.
d) Walmart.

11. I work best with others when
a) They pretend to be cheerful.
b) They do as I say.
c) They leave me alone.
d) They bring food to meetings.

12. The best team meeting is
a) One that is cancelled.
b) One where I actually get to say something.
c) One where we accomplish something.
d) One where we plan to take over the school.

Resource #4

QUESTIONNAIRE 2

Do You Really Know Your Teammates?

As you think about them, answer the following:

Which of your teammates is most likely to

1. Run, play volleyball, etc. in their spare time? ______
2. Drive a sports car if they could afford it? ______
3. Enjoy getting dressed up to go out? ______
4. Travel to exotic places for vacation? ______
5. Be in the Witness Protection Program? ______
6. Call their mom every day? ______
7. Moonlight? ______
8. Wear big fuzzy slippers at home? ______
9. Watch a lot of reality TV? ______
10. Be writing a novel in their free time? ______
11. Own a circular saw? ______
12. Plan to visit Branson, Missouri some day? ______
13. Go to movies by themselves? ______
14. While cleaning the house, play loud music and dance? ______
15. Keep Band-Aids and antiseptic in their car? ______
16. Live to be 100? ______
17. Enjoy a Monster Truck show? ______
18. Eat more sugar than protein? ______
19. Sleep less than six hours each night? ______
20. Hate this survey? ______

Resource #5

We Stand for This . . .

We care about all of our kids.
To show this . . .

. . . we will listen to and respect each other.

. . . we will assign one adult to each student to assure that each one has a personal advocate.

. . . we will discuss all our students every week to best meet their needs.

We believe young adolescents need to take responsibility for themselves and their learning.
To show this . . .

. . . we will give students real responsibilities and chances for decision-making.

We believe young adolescents learn best through engaging, exciting learning experiences.
To show this . . .

. . . we will deal with important, relevant ideas in our curriculum.

. . . we will structure activities that get kids discussing, moving, planning, and creating.

We believe that cooperative teaching leads to deeper understandings of concepts.
To show this . . .

. . . we will reinforce concepts that are common across all the disciplines.

. . . we will cooperate in planning instructional strategies.

Resource #6

The Explorers We Believe:

All the students belong to all of us.
SO each of us will be an advocate for each student.

All of our students deserve an orderly, safe, and nurturing environment in which to learn.
SO we will set rules and procedures that build and sustain such an environment. These will focus on trust and respect for one another and one another's belongings.

All students can learn. All students have gifts.
SO we will identify each student's learning gifts, styles, and needs. Then we will work with the student to design a personal learning plan that fits their learning style, abilities, and needs.

All learners need affirmation and encouragement.
SO we will select processes that the whole community will use to encourage learners. And, we will celebrate successes.

Young adolescents need to learn healthy ways to face and handle conflict.
SO we will not fear or hide from conflict. We will teach and practice ways of resolving conflicts. The adults will model healthy conflict resolution.

Resource #7

Team Dynamite

Vision

What is our goal?

During this academic year, the seventh grade Dynamite team will create a community of learners who value academic success and each other as partners in achievement.

What will we do to reach our goal?

We will hold regular team-wide meetings to build spirit and create community.

We will build a positive attitude through team identity and cooperative activities.

We will assure that students set strong academic goals for themselves and work with at least one partner to monitor the goals.

We will work tirelessly to meet each individual learner's needs.

We will avoid the negative, always focusing on the bright future each student has.

How will we know when we have succeeded?

We will see significantly less absenteeism (85% or better attendance).

We will see a significant reduction in behavioral incidents (60% or better).

We will see a high level of mastery of material (85% proficient each trimester).

We will see academic growth for the lower echelon of learners (10-15% improvement).

Resource #8, page 1

Where Are We Now?

Team Expectations	Need to Create	Need to Discuss	Need to Review	Completed
Is there a written team mission or vision (or both)?				
Are team roles and expectations established?				
Are team roles suited to each team member?				
Is there a set agenda for each meeting?				
Has the team set consistent policies and procedures for students?				
Does the team regularly discuss curriculum and instruction connections? How often?				
Has the team set a name?				
Does the team celebrate communal events and successes (for students and teachers)?				
Is homework for the week discussed by the team?				
Is a team calendar created and referenced?				
Does the team have a student information log?				
Can team members identify student workloads for the week?				

Resource #8, page 2

Where Are We Now? page 2

Team Expectations	Need to Create	Need to Discuss	Need to Review	Completed
Does the team follow up on tasks by assigning roles and responsibilities?				
Is there a set team grading policy?				
Does the team discuss issues and concerns voiced by parents and caregivers?				
Are there established norms for team meetings?				
Are outside resources used (counselors and administrators)?				
Does the team share new teaching strategies and ideas?				
Does the team read or study (or watch) books, articles, and videos together?				
Does the team spend time evaluating student work?				
Is there a process for communicating with support staff?				
Does the team document all plans, decisions, and contacts?				
Does the team have a common discipline policy and intervention plan?				
Does the team discuss strategies for advisory, flex class, or homeroom?				

Resource #9

Some Decision-Making Models

Plus & Minus Overview

Make a plus and minus column for each decision. List the pros (reasons why this is a good solution) and the cons (reasons why this might not be a good decision). When the list is finished, make the choice that has the most compelling list of pros!

Flow Chart

Identify the decision to be made. Identify two or more possible choices. Then use a visual diagram to show what events, actions, benefits, consequences, or other issues that would result from each choice. Analyze the information. It can point you to the best choice.

Multi-Voting

Each member votes on as many solutions as they like.
The solution that gets the most votes is the team decision.

Multi-Voting with a Twist

Each member has five votes—that they can divide (in any configuration) among alternate decisions. The solution that gets the most votes is the team decision.

Chart the Components

Analyze the issue and create possible outcomes to view and evaluate. First, define the issue. Then list possible decisions. For each decision, detail what the action would look like and what the consequences will be. Looking at the lists can help you choose the best option. See Resource #10 in this book.

What We Can Live With 

Each member lists what they can live with. The team chooses a decision that is on everybody's list.

Cause & Affect Chain

Consider varying possible decisions by writing them as "If . . .Then . . ." statements. This shows the results and consequences that are likely to flow from different decisions. Team members review the list of statements to see which decision has the greatest number of agreeable "Then . . ." statements.

Majority Rules

Take a straight-out vote! Follow the viewpoint of the majority—and move on.

Resource #10

Anatomy of a Decision

What's the issue or question to be decided? ______________________

____

What are the relevant facts? ______________________

____

Option 1	Option 2	Option 3
What consequences would flow from this decision?	What consequences would flow from this decision?	What consequences would flow from this decision?
______	______	______
______	______	______
______	______	______
______	______	______
______	______	______
______	______	______
What actions would follow from this decision?	What actions would follow from this decision?	What actions would follow from this decision?
______	______	______
______	______	______
______	______	______
______	______	______

Resource #11

Team Roles and Responsibilities

We agree on these roles:

Role	Responsibilities	Team Member

Top Priorities for Shared Responsibilities

Each member is responsible to each other member for:

1. ____________________
2. ____________________
3. ____________________
4. ____________________

Team ____________________ Date ______________

Resource #12

Some Team-Meeting Personalities

Sometimes the personal "agendas" or patterns of team members can delay or derail the progress of a team meeting. That's why we have a good agenda and stick to it! Here's a look at a few of the different personal styles associated with team-meeting behavior. Do you any of recognize these?
You can probably add more descriptions.

THE BULLDOZER

This person will plow right over others. They never have enough time to talk and can take over a meeting in heartbeat. They always look busy, but rarely are. They often are afraid of being placed on a school-wide committee. The Bulldozer is good at dealing with issues and making sure a task gets completed. This person is unstoppable!

The Nurturer

Nurturers feel that "eating makes a meeting." When things get difficult, they make cupcakes—and the world is a better place. They avoid conflict, yet are often involved in it in some way or another. They have been known to start a conversation by saying, "Don't tell her I said this, but ..." Their hearts are in the right place, but they sometimes go overboard or get over-involved. Nurturers are experts at dealing with parents or caregivers and students.

THE SPASTIC TEACHER

The spastic teacher is the one who unloads twenty other people from the clown car, but has no idea how the clowns got into the car. This teacher might say things like, "I am going to turn the room into an aquarium," but has no plan to make the transformation happen. Spastic teachers have the best intentions, but lack the follow-through and focus. The spastic teacher will do anything that is asked, but is really just focused on being with the kids. Do not put them in charge of ordering the bus for the field trip.

Miss Lost-in-the-Weeds Teacher

Miss Lost-in-the-Weeds walks around asking if today is the field trip. She thinks the meeting is in the library, even though everyone else is in the cafeteria. She asks the same question that was just asked and sometimes lacks focus and vision. (Note: Mister Lost-in-the-Weeds can be found on any school staff, as well.) Both are fun to be around and will make you laugh; and they will do anything for anybody. They just can't find their car keys.

Resource #13

Team Meeting Agenda

The Aviators

Team ____________________

Members Present ____________________

____

Past Business ____________________

____

____

____

____

____

Today's Business

Emergency Concerns

Action Items Decision-Action	Person(s) Responsible	Timeline

Resource #14

Team Meeting Agenda

The Dolphins

Date ______________________

Members Present - Write Initials _____ _____ _____ _____ _____

Time	Item	Decision
________ 1.		
________ 2.		
________ 3.		
________ 4.		
________ 5.		
________ 6.		

Next Steps	*Who?*	*When?*
1.		
2.		
3.		
4.		

Items for Next Agenda

Resource #15

Team Meeting Agenda

The Comets

Members Present:
Old Business Follow-up:

New Discussion:

Time	Item to Discuss	Decision	Follow-Up Who? and When?
	1.		
	2.		
	3.		
	4.		
	5.		
	6.		

Emergency Items and Logistics:

Time	Item to Discuss	Decision	Follow-Up Who? and When?
	1.		
	2.		
	3.		
	4.		

Resource #16

Examining Our Team's Current Expectations

Identify a category (such as management or academics). Write procedures in that category that are part of your classroom processes (for example, cell phone use or leaving the room during class). Then each teacher on the team briefly describes their expectations or rules for that procedure. Compare the different expectations.

Category:

Procedure/Topic Expectation	Expectation Teacher 1:__________	Expectation Teacher 2:__________	Expectation Teacher 3:__________	Expectation Teacher 4:__________

Resource #17

Our Team Protocols

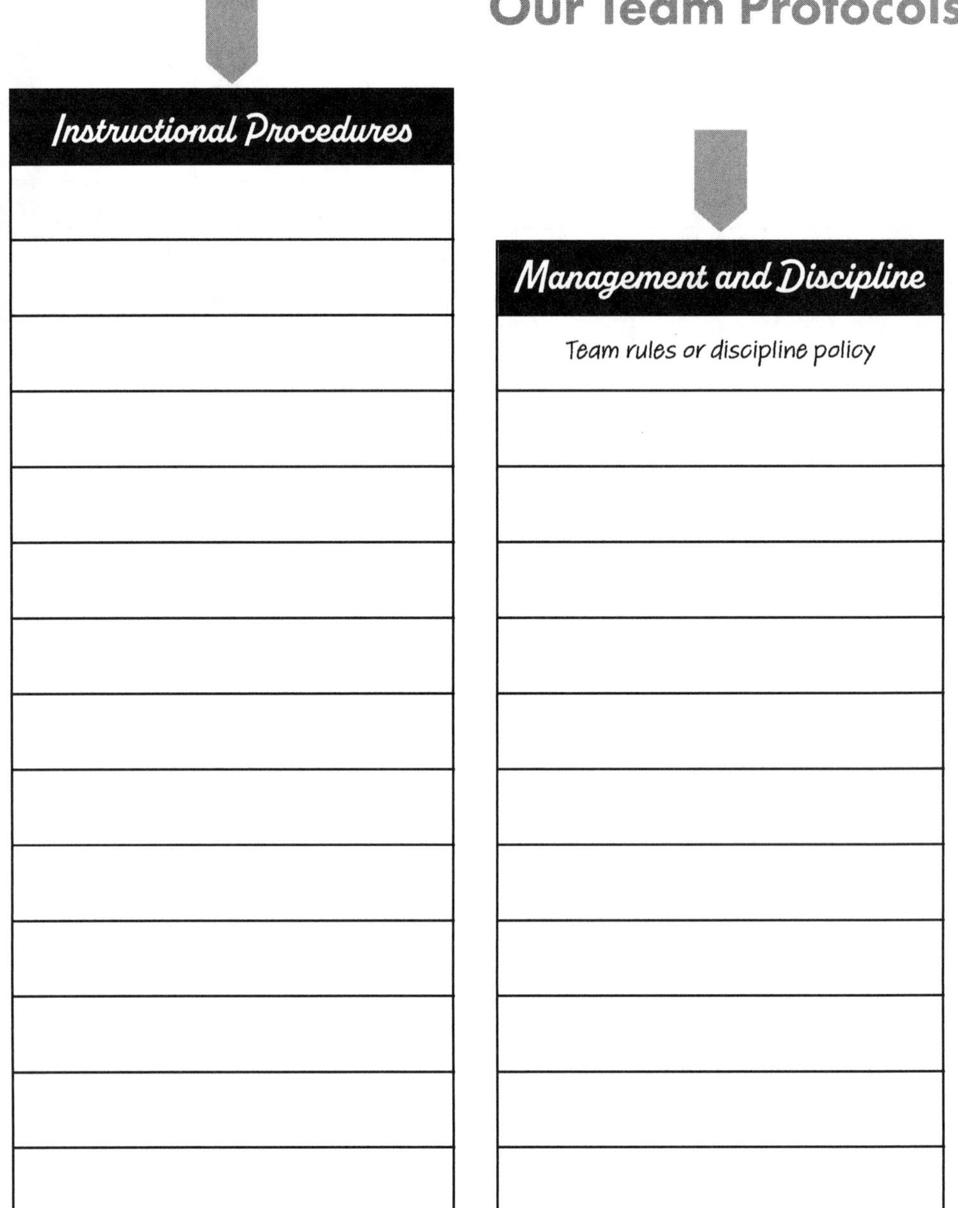

Resource #18

TIPS Planning Form

(Team Intervention Plan for Students)

For ____________________ Team ____________________ Date ____________

3 Issues

1

2

3

5 Strategies for moving forward

1

2

3

4

5

3 Ways to Follow Up

1

2

3

2 Rewards

1

2

Student Signature ____________________

Parent or Caregiver Signature ____________________

Teacher Signature ____________________

Resource #19 page 1

LOOKING AT ALL THE FACTORS THAT AFFECT STUDENTS

CONSIDER ALL OF THESE AREAS WHEN CREATING INTERVENTION PLANS (TIPS)

Social Issues *Questions to consider:*	*Emotional Issues* *Questions to consider:*	*Academic Issues* *Questions to consider:*	*Behavioral Issues* *Questions to consider:*	*Developmental Issues* *Questions to consider:*	*Outside Influences* *Questions to consider:*
• How does the student relate to peers? • Is the student able to work in a group? • Is the student mature for their age socially, or lacking basic social skills? • Is there another student who works well with this student? • Are there rewards that allow the student to spend time with friends?	• How does the student react to praise or when corrected for bad behaviors? • Is the student quick to anger or passive aggressive? • Is the student prone to crying or other emotional outbursts? • Does the student need praise and constant support? • What methods get the student to respond in a positive manner?	• What information can you gather from the student's past test scores? • What are the areas of academic concern for this student? • In what specific skills has the student not shown proficiency? • What about grades? • What about missing work?	• How many referrals have been sent on this student? • What are their major behavioral issues? • What sets the student off—triggers inappropriate behavior? • Is the student aggressive? • What methods have worked to help the student with behavior?	• Is the student a concrete learner? • Does the student relate to abstract thoughts? • How are the student's motor skills? • Can they relate to shades of gray? • Can they identify their actions and relate to consequences?	• Has the student had issues from outside that affect school work? • Does the student have support at home? • Is the student able to do homework in a safe, secure environment? • Do parents and caregivers follow through on plans and teacher ideas? • Are there issues related to medication or evidence of abuse or trauma? • Is counseling or other support provided for the student or family? • Have there been recent death, divorce, or health issues in the family?

Resource #19 page 2

Student ______________________ Date __________

LOOKING AT ALL THE FACTORS THAT AFFECT STUDENTS, page 2

CONSIDER ALL OF THESE AREAS WHEN CREATING INTERVENTION PLANS (TIPS)

Social Issues	Emotional Issues	Academic Issues	Behavioral Issues	Developmental Issues	Outside Influences
Notes:	Notes:	Notes:	Notes:	Notes:	Notes:

Resource #20

IDEAS for TIPS Action Plans

Team Intervention Strategies

Here are some suggestions to get your team started building your lists.
Use them as inspiration to add strategies that fit your students and your needs.

Behavioral Strategies

- Self-monitoring checklist for student
- Student services assistance
- Twice a week quick-check at team meeting
- Twice-a-week quick-check with parent or caregiver
- Signed daily progress report
- Alternate location for some of the school work
- Punch card for progress
- Teacher signals to help with behavior
- Daily self-report to advocate
- Student-suggested strategy

Academic Strategies

- Phone conference with parent or caregiver
- Daily progress report of grades and progress
- Use of a peer tutor
- Reduce or break-up assignments
- After-school assistance with assignments
- Weekly assistance with organization
- Verbal checks for understanding
- Alternative assessments offered
- Student-generated strategy ideas
- Daily practice of skill or process
- Daily check of student planner
- Daily progress report or signed daily agenda
- Home or private tutoring
- Alternate learning settings considered

Follow-Up Ideas

- Student progress report in team meeting
- Check in with a parent or caregiver
- Create a long-term self-monitoring checklist for student
- Student self-report on prescribed schedule
- Check in with teacher twice a week after school

Rewards

- Lunch in classroom with selected friends
- 15 minutes of game of choice, drawing time, creating a video
- Student choice (approval by teacher)
- Homework by-pass

Resource #21

The Index Card Activity

Guidelines for Assigning an Advocate to Each Student on the Team

Team ______________________ Date ______________

Step One

Put each student's first and last name on an index card. Print in large letters.
OR, have students make a name card as a Getting-to-Know-You activity.

Step Two

Place all the cards on the table, face up, with every name visible.

Step Three

The most experienced teacher on the team picks one student card.

Step Four

The teacher explains the choice.

Step Five

The next most experienced teacher picks a card and explains the choice. The other team members pick cards and explain choices. Repeat this three times for each team member.

Step Six

Complete several speed rounds—each teacher picks three names per turn (three or four rounds). Explanations are optional. Do this until there are about 20 cards left on the table.

Step Seven

Once there are about 20 cards left, stop. Each teacher looks at the student names they have chosen, examining them for patterns in the characteristics. Then, the entire team takes a collective look at the remaining cards, considering why these students have not yet been selected.

Step Eight

Considering the remaining cards one by one, the team asks, "What does this student need?" After discussion, the team decides who will take each of these names.

Step Nine

Each teacher is the assigned advocate for the students named on the chosen cards. The teacher will make regular connections with these kids and keep a general overview for each, with actions the team has planned for advocacy.

Resource #22

Thumbs Up, Thumbs Down

Checking on Student Academic Success

Step One

Schedule time in two or three meetings over the quarter to check on a specific topic or behavior related to students' success with their schoolwork. Plan the first meeting for about 3 weeks into the quarter. Plan the second meeting about 2 to 3 weeks later, and the third about 2 weeks before the end of the quarter. An easy way to remember these times are to think of the check-ups as Weeks 3, 5, and 7! Agree on the topic at the time you schedule the meeting. Then each teacher can come to the meeting with intervention strategy ideas for how they can help students solve whatever problem is targeted.

Step Two

Prepare an alphabetical list of all the students on the team. You'll need three of these for each quarter, so you might prepare several lists! Remind teachers to bring grade books or other records from their classes that supply information about students' academic status.

Step Three

With the entire team of teachers gathered, say each name out loud in order. Give the student a **thumbs up** if they are doing okay with the topic you've chosen. If a student is **not** doing well with the chosen topic, you give them a **thumbs down**.

Step Four

If only one teacher has given thumbs down, that teacher selects intervention strategies for the student. However, if the student has multiple thumbs-down responses, their name goes on a list of students who need some intervention.

Step Five

Once the team has made the list of students who need attention for this issue, the team chooses strategies to help students on the list address and solve the issue.

Resource #23

Academic-Success-Check, Team Record

Checking on Student Academic Success

Team ______________________ Dates ______________

Quarter	1	2	3	4
Week	3	5	7	

Topic for Check-Up ____

Student	Intervention Strategy	Who Oversees?	Follow-Up Comments

Resource #24

Ways to Connect Curriculum

In order to connect curriculum, teams must have a comprehensive understanding of the course of study in each core area. This requires ongoing conversation and sharing. In planning to connect curriculum to any extent, think about the topics and ideas you will connect. But think beyond that, as well, to the many other facets that are part of "doing" your curriculum across the team. Here are some suggestions. Add your ideas to these lists.

Look for concepts and themes that are relevant and critical across the subject areas. Point out to students how these ideas show up again and again in all the disciplines.

Examples:

- Change
- Risk
- Movement
- Patterns and systems
- Cycles
- Rules
- Structure
- Order and organization
- Authority
- Boundaries
- Scarcity
- Resources
- Transitions
- Resistance to change
- Causes and Effects

Look for skills and processes that are needed across the disciplines. Agree on common formats and expectations for students to create, learn, or use these. As much as possible, correlate your schedules to use the skills during the same time period.

Examples:

- Note-taking
- Deep reading
- Critical thinking
- Essay-writing
- Vocabulary mastery
- Summarizing
- Paraphrasing
- Predicting
- Preparing and giving a speech
- Reading maps, charts, tables, graphs
- Reflecting
- Evaluating
- Creating visual presentations
- Utilizing various digital tools and applications

Resource #25

10-Day Learning Goals

Team ______________________ Dates ______________ through ______________

Name each goal, give a quick explanation for why it is needed, and plan for how teachers will implement the goal. After the 10 days, do a quick evaluation of how the team did at meeting the goal. Or, ask the students to complete the "How did we do?" reflection.

Academic Goal

____

____

Why it's needed: ______________________________

____

How teachers will implement it:

____

How did we do?

- ☐ We rocked it!
- ☐ We're almost there.
- ☐ We need more practice

Suggestion for next goal:

Non-Academic Goal

____

____

Why it's needed: ______________________________

____

How teachers will implement it:

____

How did we do?

- ☐ We rocked it!
- ☐ We're almost there.
- ☐ We need more practice

Suggestion for next goal:

Resource #26, page 1

Some Reflections on Our Team

Circle the response that most accurately describes your team.

1. **Our team meets**
   At least 3 times a week.
   At least 3 times a month.
   At least 3 times a semester.
   At least 3 it meets.

2. **When we refer to students on our team, we**
   Call them by name.
   Call them names.
   Use "what's his name."
   Use nicknames ("Mr. Bigmouth," "Ms Goth Beauty").

3. **For professional development (PD), our team**
   Sends a team member to a conference every few years.
   Has a regular day scheduled for PD.
   Read an article once.
   Thinks PD means "Puberty Development" and refers it to the counselor.

4. **Our team has common goals, including**
   Getting through the year.
   Getting through the year without hurting each other.
   Getting through to the students.
   Making specific plans for student success.

5. **Our team regularly looks at data in order to**
   Seem smarter than we are.
   Please the administration.
   Help us with Sudoku.
   Work together to strategize areas where students need help.

6. **When teams collaborate regarding curriculum and instruction**
   Everything gets garbled.
   Kids get time off.
   Kids make better academic connections.
   Teachers take turns teaching.

7. **Our team communicates with our students' families by**
   Website.
   Emails.
   Pigeon.
   Parent nights.

Resource #26, page 2

8 **Teams allow students to have a choice in their own learning because**
Teachers are more motivated.
Kids have less to do.
Teachers don't know as much as kids.
Kids today are more independent.

9 **When my team meeting is scheduled to begin**
I am in my seat eating the first piece of cake.
I arrive fashionably late.
I am ready with required materials.
I am busy elsewhere.

10 **I am working on a team because**
It gives me less work to do.
I like the food at the meetings.
I know it is great for kids.
I am basically a sad, lonely person.

11 **Our team communicates with other teams in our school or grade**
When they do something we don't like.
Whenever we distribute our team minutes, so everyone knows what's up.
Whenever we want to suck up to the administration.
Whenever we challenge them to a rumble in the faculty lounge.

12 **When it comes to disciplining students on our team**
We rely on the principal.
We rely on our common discipline process.
We rely on the guillotine.
We rely on prayer.

13 **An example of common policies and procedures on our team is**
We don't allow anything.
No shirt, no shoes? No sit at desk!
We have common requirements for late work.
We are not late to work.

14 **We share responsibilities on our team by**
Taking turns bringing food.
Taking turns chairing the meeting and preparing the agenda.
Taking turns as lookout in case the principal comes.
Taking turns badmouthing the students.

15 **As part of our teaming effort, we celebrate with our students**
Especially on their days off.
Especially when we are tired.
Especially when they have success.
Especially when a parent sends brownies.

Resource #27

Ideas for Team Professional Development

Keep building this list by adding your own ideas and needs that arise.

Do Together

- Read, watch, and listen together; then discuss (article, blog, podcast, video, guest speaker)
- Bring in an expert on any topic (someone from inside or outside your school)
- Identify each team member's topic or skill of expertise and teach each other
- Share and demonstrate best practices
- Videotape yourself teaching; bring it to the team for feedback
- Practice any new strategy; try it out on each other
- Examine student work together; discuss what it teaches you
- Plan ways to teach specific cross-discipline skills; try them out together
- Polish your effective questioning techniques
- Evaluate your team dynamics

Learn More About

- Better partnerships with students' families
- Bias—explicit and unintentional
- Use of community resources
- Classroom management and climate
- Discipline intervention strategies
- Academic vocabulary
- Content-area literacy and numeracy
- Digital citizenship, safety, and self-control
- Virtual learning and blended learning
- Gamification
- Restorative practices
- Strategies for engagement and motivation
- Reaching deeply disengaged students
- Differentiated learning strategies
- Understanding students' emotions
- Helping students overcome trauma
- Fostering resilience
- Any number of SEL topics
- Using student data
- Collaborative learning (groupwork)
- Independent study
- Student voice and choice
- Formative assessment
- Scoring assignments; grading consistency
- Technology use
- Self-care, work-life balance for teachers
- Teacher morale
- Teacher relationships with administration, school board, community
- Student-led conferences
- Major issues challenging middle school kids, for example:
  - Social media use, misuse, and dangers
  - Gender identity
  - Questions of sexuality
  - Racial inequality
  - Discrimination of any kind for any reason
  - Anxiety and depression
  - Poverty
  - Pressure from peers, families, and society
  - Drug or alcohol use
  - Risky sexual activity
  - Harassment, online and off
  - Body image problems
  - Violence in the community
  - School safety

Resource #28

OUR Team PD Menu and Timeline

Month	Topics or Activities	Who Leads?	Done? Date?	Comments or Further Plans

Team ____________________ Date ____________

Endnotes

1. Bishop, P. A., & Harrison, L. M. (2021).) *The successful middle school: This we believe.* Columbus: OH: Association for Middle Level Education.
2. Perez, A. M. (2021). *The successful middle school schedule.* Columbus, OH: Association for Middle Level Education.
3. Bishop, P. A., & Harrison, L. M. (2022). *The successful middle school: This we believe* (p. 51). Columbus, OH: Association for Middle Level Education.
4. Bishop, P. A., & Harrison, L. M. (2021). *The successful middle school: This we believe.* (p. 51). Columbus, OH: Association for Middle Level Education.
5. Arhar, J. (1990). Interdisciplinary teaming as a school intervention to increase the social bonding of middle level students. *Research in Middle Level Education: Selected Studies 1990.* National Middle School Association.
6. Boyle, S. J., & Bishop, P. A. (2004). Young adolescent voices: Students' perceptions of interdisciplinary teaming. *RMLE Online 28*(1). https://www.tandfonline.com/doi/pdf/10.1080/19404476.2004.11658176?
7. Felner, R. D., Jackson, A. W., Kasak, D., Mulhall, P. F., Brand, S., & Flowers, N. (1997). The impact of school reform in the middle years: Longitudinal study of a network engaged in Turning Points-based comprehensive school transformation. *Phi Delta Kappan, 78*(7), 528-532, 541-550.
8. Felner, R., Mertens, S., & Lipsitz, J. (1996). *Assessment of middle grades education in Michigan: A report to the W. K. Kellogg Foundation's Middle Start Initiative.* Urbana, IL: University of Illinois.
9. Flowers, N. (2000). How teaming influences classroom practices (2000). *Middle School Journal, 32*(2), 52-59.
10. Flowers, N., Mertens, S. B., & Mulhall, P. F. (1999). The impact of teaming: Five research-based outcomes. *Middle School Journal, 31*(2), 57-60.

11. Flowers, N., Mertens, S. B., & Mulhall, P. F. (2003). Lessons learned from more than a decade of middle grades research. *Middle School Journal, 35*(2), 55-59.
12. Mertens, S. B., & Flowers, N. (2003). Middle school practices improve student achievement in high poverty schools. *Middle School Journal, 35*(1), 33-43.
13. Flowers, N. (2000). How teaming influences classroom practices. *Middle School Journal, 32*(2), 52-59.
14. Flowers, N. (2000). How teaming influences classroom practices. *Middle School Journal, 32*(2), 52-59.
15. Flowers, N., Mertens, S. B., & Mulhall, P. F. (2000) What makes interdisciplinary teams effective? *Middle School Journal, 37*(4), 53-56.
16. Flowers, N., Mertens, S. B., & Mulhall, P. F. (2003). Lessons learned from more than a decade of middle grades research. *Middle School Journal, 35*(2), 55-59.
17. Warren, L. L., & Muth, K. D. (1995). The impact of common planning time on middle grade students and teachers. *Research in Middle Level Education Quarterly, 18*(3), 41-58.
18. Perez, A. M. (2021). *The successful middle school schedule.* Columbus, OH: Association for Middle Level Education.
19. Felner, R. D., Jackson, A. W., Kasak, D., Mulhall, P., Brand, S., & Flowers, N. (1997). The impact of school reform in the middle years: Longitudinal study of a network engaged in Turning Points-based comprehensive school transformation. *Phi Delta Kappan, 78*(7), 528-532, 541-550.
20. Flowers, N., Mertens, S. B., & Mulhall, P. F. (1999). The impact of teaming: Five research-based outcomes. *Middle School Journal, 31*(2), 57-60.
21. Flowers, N., Mertens, S. B., & Mulhall, P F. (2000). What makes interdisciplinary teams effective? *Middle School Journal, 37*(4), 53-56.
22. Flowers, N., Mertens, S. B., & Mulhall, P. F. (2003). Lessons learned from more than a decade of middle grades research. *Middle School Journal, 35*(2), 55-59.
23. Hunter, W., Jasper, A. D., & Williamson, R. L. (2014). Utilizing middle school common planning time to support inclusive environments. *Intervention in School and Clinic, 50*(2), 114-120.
24. Mertens, S. B., & Flowers, N. (2003). Middle school practices improve student achievement in high poverty schools. *Middle School Journal, 35*(1), 33-43.
25. Mertens, S. B., & Flowers, N. (2006). Middle Start's impact on comprehensive middle school reform. *Middle Grades Research Journal, 1*(1), 1-26.

26. Warren, L. L., & Muth, K. D. (1995). The impact of common planning time on middle grade students and teachers. *Research in Middle Level Education Quarterly, 18*(3),41-58.
27. Flowers, N. (2000). How teaming influences classroom practices. *Middle School Journal, 32*(2), 52-59.
28. Bishop, P. A., & Harrison, L. M. (2021). *The successful middle school: This we believe.* Columbus: OH: Association for Middle Level Education.
29. Silver, D. (2012) *Fall down 7 times get up 8: Teaching kids to succeed* (pp. 99-112). Thousand Oaks, CA: Corwin.
30. Bromberg-Martin, E. S., Matsumoto, M. & Hirosaka, O. (2010). Dopamine in motivational control: Rewarding, aversive, and alerting. *Neuron, 66*(5), 815-834.
31. Bishop, P. A., & Harrison, L. M. (2021). *The successful middle school: This we believe* (pp. 15-16). Columbus: OH: Association for Middle Level Education.
32. Quin, D. (2016). Longitudinal and contextual associations between teacher-student relationships and student engagement: A systematic review. *Review of Educational Research,* 87(2), 345-387.
33. Ladd, G. W. (1999). Peer relationships and social competence during early and middle childhood. *Annual Review of Psychology 50*, 333–359.
34. Ybing, L., Lynch, A. D., Kalvin, C, Liu, J., & Lerner, J. (2011). Peer relationships as a context for the development of school engagement. *International Journal of Behavioral Development, 35*(4), 329-342.
35. Steinberg, L., & Monahan, K. C. (2007). Age differences in resistance to peer influence. *Developmental Psychology, 43*(6), 1531-1543.
36. Flowers, N. (2000). How teaming influences classroom practices. *Middle School Journal, 32*(2), 52-59.
37. Mertens, S., Flowers, N., & Mulhall, P. (1998). *The Middle Start Initiative, Phase I: A longitudinal analysis of Michigan middle-level schools.* Urbana, IL: University of Illinois.
38. Perez, A. M. (2021). *The successful middle school schedule* (pp. 16-21). Columbus, OH: Association for Middle Level Education.